Mastering Professional
Help Desk Skills

A Comprehensive Guide for Customer Service Excellence

Gerard Assey

Mastering Professional Help Desk Skills
A Comprehensive Guide for Customer Service Excellence

By
Gerard Assey
© Copyright 2024 by Author

Published by:
Gerard Assey
19/18, Palli Arasan Street
Anna Nagar East
Chennai - 600 102

ISBN: 978-81-971121-3-3

(Image courtesy Freepik: www.Freepik.com-Thank You)

Table of Contents

Preface
Crafting Lasting Impressions in Customer Service
The Importance of Customer Service
Key Benefits of Providing Excellent Customer Service
The Roles, Responsibilities & Functions of a HELP DESK Professional
KEY Attributes, Traits and Qualities of Help Desk Professionals

Telephone Techniques and Skills
Pre-Call Planning and Preparation
During the Call: Steps to a Professional Service Call
Effective Questioning and Listening Skills
Open-ended Questions to get to the Root of Issues in Various Categories of Industries
Steps to be a Good Listener
Handling Complaints and Angry Customers
Resolving Complaints Effectively
Empowering Frontline Staff to Resolve Issues

Personal (Face to Face) Interaction
Ensuring Proper Grooming and Presenting a Professional Image
Customer Care Skills

Internet Interaction (Email)
Professional DO's & DON'T's of Emailing

Continuous Improvement and Teamwork
Coping with Stress in the Service Industry
Teamwork in Customer Service

Understanding Customer Behavior
A Personality Assessment for Customer Service Staff
Identifying Different Customer Types
Managing Difficult People and Sensitive Situations

Understanding Users and Categorizing Them
Typical Incident Management Process
Implementing a Successful Help Desk Skills Initiative: Action Plan

Empowering Help Desk Professionals for Excellence in Customer Service

Conclusion: Elevating Your Helpdesk Journey
About the Author

Preface

Welcome to the world of **'Mastering Professional Help Desk Skills:** *A Comprehensive Guide for Customer Service Excellence.'* As we navigate the intricate landscape of modern customer service, the role of help desk professionals becomes increasingly vital. In the realm where "people make 90% of their lasting impression in the first 90 seconds," the skills possessed by these professionals not only shape the immediate interactions but lay the foundation for enduring customer relationships.

This book is a comprehensive guide meticulously crafted to empower help desk personnel, customer service representatives, and CS Engineers with the essential skills required to excel in the dynamic and challenging environments of personal, telephone, and internet interactions. The importance of the first point of contact cannot be overstated, and our aim is to equip you with the knowledge and expertise to make those initial moments count.

In a world where customer loyalty is a currency of immense value, the significance of effective customer service cannot be overstressed. We delve into not only the technical aspects but also the art of building genuine connections. With insights drawn from real-world experiences and industry best practices, this book is not just a manual; it's a companion on your journey towards becoming a customer service maestro.

Why This Book Matters

The statistics speak for themselves – businesses losing customers due to dissatisfaction, the cost disparity between acquiring new customers and retaining existing ones, and the undeniable truth that excellent service is not just a competitive weapon but a survival skill in today's service-oriented economy. This book is a response to these challenges, a roadmap to navigate the intricacies of customer interactions, and a toolbox filled with strategies to not only meet but exceed customer expectations.

What You'll Find Inside

From mastering telephone techniques to excelling in personal interactions and navigating the nuances of internet communication, each chapter is designed to hone specific skills. The Diamond Rule of Service, the C.A.R.E. Principle, and the intricacies of complaint handling – these are not just theoretical concepts but practical tools you can wield to enhance your professional repertoire.

We go beyond the technicalities, emphasizing the importance of attitude, stress management, and continuous improvement. The journey towards becoming a customer service champion involves not just following a set of guidelines but embodying a mindset that puts the customer at the center.

How to Use This Book

This book is structured to guide you systematically through the multifaceted world of customer service. Each chapter provides a deep dive into specific aspects, offering actionable insights, real-world examples, and practical exercises. Whether you're a seasoned professional looking to refine your skills or someone entering the field with wide-eyed enthusiasm, there's something here for everyone.

Your Journey Begins Here

Embark on this journey with an open mind and a commitment to excellence. Let the pages ahead be your companion in developing the skills that will not only make you an indispensable asset to your organization but will also set you apart in a world where exceptional service is the key to success.

Thank you for choosing to explore the nuances of Professional Helpdesk Skills with us.
May this journey be as enriching for you as it has been for us in bringing this guide to life.

Crafting Lasting Impressions in Customer Service

In the fast-paced world of customer service, where impressions are formed in mere seconds, the timeless wisdom encapsulated in the statement, "People make 90% of their lasting impression in the first 90 seconds," carries profound weight. This observation, while universally applicable, holds particular significance for the dedicated professionals manning the help desk - the unsung heroes responsible for the initial touchpoints with customers. The gravity of these moments cannot be overstated. Whether the encounter is face-to-face, over the phone, or through the digital channels of the internet, it serves as a pivotal juncture where the perception of a company is etched into the customer's consciousness. It's a critical handshake, a virtual greeting, or a friendly voice on the line that lays the foundation for the entire customer experience.

In the realm of customer service, the help desk professional is the ambassador of the company, bearing the responsibility of not only addressing concerns but also creating an atmosphere of trust and reliability. The customer's journey begins with this initial contact, and the impressions formed during these moments resonate throughout the entire interaction.

Consider the scenario of a face-to-face interaction - the welcoming smile, the poised demeanor, and the attentiveness to the customer's needs. These elements collectively contribute to an environment where the customer feels valued and understood. Similarly, over the phone, the tone of voice, the ability to listen actively, and the assurance conveyed play pivotal roles in shaping the customer's perception. Even in the digital realm of emails, where words on a screen replace physical presence, the choice of language, the promptness of response, and the overall professionalism leave a lasting mark.

This comprehensive guide is meticulously curated to empower help desk and customer service personnel, including the technically proficient CS Engineers, with the indispensable skills necessary to excel across all dimensions of customer interaction. From the warmth of face-to-face encounters to the finesse required in telephonic conversations and the nuances of digital communication via email, each mode demands a unique set of skills, all of which are essential components of delivering exceptional customer service.

As we delve into the subsequent chapters, we will embark on a journey to dissect and master the intricacies of personal interactions, telephone etiquettes, and internet communication. The objective is clear - to equip professionals with the expertise needed not just to meet customer expectations but to exceed them. In doing so, we aim to transform the help desk from a mere point of query resolution to a beacon of positive experiences, thereby solidifying the company's standing in the eyes of its customers.

The Importance of Customer Service

Customer service stands as the bedrock of any successful business. In this chapter, we delve into the profound impact that customer service has on a company's success, emphasizing the critical role of first impressions and the enduring importance of customer retention and loyalty.

The Impact of First Impressions

Significance of Initial Contact

The adage "People make 90% of their lasting impression in the first 90 seconds" holds timeless wisdom, particularly in customer service. The initial contact between a customer and a company sets the tone for the entire relationship. Consider the scenario of a customer walking into a retail store. The warmth of the greeting, the attentiveness of the staff, and the overall atmosphere form an immediate impression. This impression, whether positive or negative, lingers in the customer's mind and influences their perception of the brand.

To illustrate, imagine two scenarios: In the first, a customer enters a store and is greeted by a smiling, well-presented staff member who offers assistance. In the second, the customer experiences indifference and a lack of engagement. In both instances, the first 90 seconds play a decisive role in shaping the customer's view of the business.

Customer Perception and Company Success

Customer perception is not merely a fleeting sentiment; it directly correlates with the success of the company. Positive initial impressions lead to enhanced customer trust, loyalty, and advocacy. Conversely, negative impressions can result in lost business and tarnished reputations. In the age of social media and online reviews, a single negative experience can reverberate across a vast audience, underscoring the enduring impact of these initial moments.

Consider the well-documented case of Zappos, the online shoe and clothing retailer. Zappos has built its brand on exceptional customer service, often going above and beyond expectations. Their commitment to creating positive first impressions has not only garnered customer loyalty but has contributed significantly to their success as a customer-centric business.

Customer Retention and Loyalty
Statistics on Customer Dissatisfaction

Understanding the landscape of customer dissatisfaction is essential. Studies consistently show that a dissatisfied customer is more likely to share their negative experience than a satisfied one. This phenomenon underscores the imperative of providing outstanding service from the outset to mitigate dissatisfaction and negative word-of-mouth.

For example, a survey conducted by Zendesk revealed that 95% of customers share bad experiences with others, compared to 87% who share good experiences. Such statistics underscore the financial implications of customer dissatisfaction and the pivotal role that exceptional service plays in mitigating these risks.

The Cost of Acquiring New Customers vs. Retaining Existing Ones

Acquiring new customers is a substantial investment, both in terms of time and resources. However, the cost of retaining existing customers is comparatively lower. Research consistently demonstrates that it is more cost-effective to keep current customers than to attract new ones. The relationship between cost and retention highlights the financial wisdom in prioritizing customer loyalty.

An illustrative example is the airline industry, where loyalty programs are designed to retain frequent fliers. Offering perks such as priority boarding, lounge access, and discounted fares fosters a sense of loyalty among customers. The airline understands that the cost of retaining a loyal customer is significantly lower than acquiring a new one.

The Diamond Rule of Service: Treating Others as You Want to be Treated

The Diamond Rule encapsulates the essence of exceptional customer service - treating others as you want to be treated. It transcends transactions and transforms customer interactions into memorable experiences. By understanding and empathizing with the customer's needs, companies can foster trust and loyalty.

Consider the example of Nordstrom, a renowned department store. Nordstrom's commitment to the Diamond Rule is legendary. Their liberal return policy, personalized service, and customer-centric approach have become synonymous with the brand. In adhering to the principle of treating customers as they would like to be treated, Nordstrom has cultivated a fiercely loyal customer base.

In conclusion, this chapter underscores the pivotal role of customer service in shaping company success. The impact of first impressions resonates throughout the customer journey, from the initial contact to long-term loyalty. By understanding the significance of these moments, implementing strategic retention practices, and embracing the Diamond Rule, businesses can elevate customer service from a transactional necessity to a competitive advantage. The subsequent chapters will delve deeper into the strategies and action plans necessary to embody these principles across personal, telephonic, and digital interactions.

Key Benefits of Providing Excellent Customer Service

Here are the several key benefits of providing Excellent Customer Service:

- ✓ **Customer Loyalty and Retention:**
  Example: A grocery store that consistently provides excellent customer service, such as helpful staff, efficient checkout processes, and personalized offers, is likely to retain customers who prefer the positive experience.
- ✓ **Positive Word-of-Mouth and Reputation:**
  Example: A satisfied customer is likely to share their positive experience with friends and family, contributing to positive word-of-mouth. This, in turn, enhances the company's reputation in the community and industry.
- ✓ **Increased Customer Lifetime Value:**
  Example: An online subscription service that goes the extra mile in customer support, addressing issues promptly and providing additional value, is likely to retain customers for a longer period, thus increasing their lifetime value to the business.
- ✓ **Differentiation in a Competitive Market:**
  Example: In a competitive market, a company known for exceptional customer service stands out. For instance, a tech company that offers personalized customer support and assistance in setting up devices differentiates itself from competitors.
- ✓ **Customer Satisfaction and Happiness:**
  Example: A hotel that consistently exceeds guest expectations in terms of service,

cleanliness, and responsiveness ensures high customer satisfaction, leading to happy guests who are more likely to return.

- ✓ **Increased Revenue and Cross-Selling Opportunities:**
  Example: A retail store that provides a positive shopping experience and understands customer preferences is well-positioned to recommend complementary products, leading to increased sales and cross-selling opportunities.
- ✓ **Brand Advocacy:**
  Example: An e-commerce platform with a user-friendly interface and responsive customer service fosters brand advocates who not only make repeat purchases but also actively recommend the platform to others.
- ✓ **Reduced Customer Churn:**
  Example: A telecommunications company that prioritizes quick issue resolution and provides incentives for customer loyalty experiences reduced customer churn, leading to a more stable customer base.

Repercussions of Not Providing Excellent Customer Service:
- ✓ **Customer Dissatisfaction:**
  Example: A restaurant with slow service, rude staff, and inconsistent food quality is likely to leave customers dissatisfied, leading to negative reviews and reduced repeat business.
- ✓ **Negative Word-of-Mouth:**
  Example: A dissatisfied customer sharing their poor experience on social media can quickly

lead to negative word-of-mouth, impacting the reputation of the business.

✓ **Loss of Customer Trust:**
Example: A financial institution that mishandles customer transactions, leading to financial losses, erodes trust and confidence in the institution's reliability.

✓ **Decreased Customer Loyalty:**
Example: An e-commerce platform with a complicated return process and unresponsive customer service may lose customer loyalty, as users seek alternatives that provide better support.

✓ **Increased Customer Churn:**
Example: A subscription-based service that consistently fails to address customer concerns may experience a high rate of customer churn, resulting in revenue loss.

✓ **Impact on Brand Image:**
Example: A company known for poor customer service may suffer from a damaged brand image, impacting its ability to attract new customers and retain existing ones.

✓ **Reduced Revenue and Missed Opportunities:**
Example: A retail store with disinterested staff and inefficient checkout processes may experience reduced foot traffic and missed opportunities for upselling or cross-selling.

✓ **Legal Consequences:**
Example: A healthcare provider that neglects patient complaints and concerns may face legal consequences for malpractice or negligence, damaging its reputation and financial standing.

In summary, the benefits of providing excellent customer service extend beyond immediate financial gains, contributing to long-term success, customer loyalty, and positive brand perception. On the flip side, neglecting customer service can have severe repercussions, affecting the bottom line, brand image, and overall sustainability of a business.

The Roles, Responsibilities & Functions of a HELP DESK Professional

Help Desk Professionals play a critical role in ensuring effective communication and support between an organization and its customers or internal users. Their responsibilities encompass a wide range of functions, from technical problem-solving to providing exceptional customer service. Below is a detailed list of roles, responsibilities, and functions of a Help Desk Professional, along with examples:

Roles and Responsibilities:

1. Customer Support:

Role: Serve as the first point of contact for customers or internal users seeking assistance with technical issues.

Responsibilities:

- ✓ Respond promptly to customer inquiries.
- ✓ Diagnose and troubleshoot technical problems.
- ✓ Provide step-by-step guidance for issue resolution.
- ✓ Ensure customer satisfaction through effective communication.

2. Technical Troubleshooting:

Role: Identify, analyze, and resolve technical issues reported by users.

Responsibilities:

- ✓ Analyze error messages and system logs.
- ✓ Utilize knowledge base and resources for issue resolution.

✓ Escalate complex problems to higher-tier support when necessary.
✓ Follow up with users to ensure issues are fully resolved.

3. Ticket Management:

Role: Efficiently manage and document support requests using a ticketing system.
Responsibilities:
✓ Create and update tickets with relevant details.
✓ Prioritize and categorize tickets based on urgency and impact.
✓ Ensure timely resolution and closure of tickets.
✓ Provide clear and concise information for future reference.

4. Communication and Interpersonal Skills:

Role: Communicate effectively with users, team members, and other departments.
Responsibilities:
✓ Clearly articulate technical information to non-technical users.
✓ Demonstrate empathy and active listening.
✓ Keep users informed about the status of their requests.
✓ Collaborate with other teams for issue resolution.

5. User Training and Guidance:

Role: Educate users on system functionalities and best practices.
Responsibilities:
✓ Conduct training sessions for new features or tools.
✓ Create user-friendly guides and documentation.

✓ Address common user errors through proactive guidance.
✓ Foster self-service options for routine issues.

6. Continuous Improvement:

Role: Contribute to the enhancement of support processes and resources.
Responsibilities:
✓ Provide feedback on recurring issues for process improvement.
✓ Suggest updates to knowledge base articles.
✓ Stay updated on industry best practices.
✓ Participate in training programs for skill development.

7. Security Awareness:

Role: Be vigilant for security-related issues and educate users on security best practices.
Responsibilities:
✓ Identify and report potential security threats.
✓ Educate users on password management and data protection.
✓ Collaborate with IT security teams for immediate responses.

8. Documentation:

Role: Maintain accurate records and documentation of support activities.
Responsibilities:
✓ Document troubleshooting steps for common issues.
✓ Update knowledge base articles with new information.
✓ Create comprehensive reports on recurring problems.
✓ Ensure the accuracy of user profiles and system configurations.

9. Team Collaboration:

Role: Work collaboratively with other help desk professionals and IT teams.
Responsibilities:
- ✓ Share knowledge and insights with team members.
- ✓ Collaborate on complex issues that require collective expertise.
- ✓ Contribute to a positive team culture.
- ✓ Provide backup support during peak times.

10. Remote Support:

Role: Provide assistance to users remotely, especially in the context of remote work environments.
Responsibilities:
- ✓ Utilize remote desktop tools for troubleshooting.
- ✓ Guide users through technical processes via phone or online chat.
- ✓ Ensure a seamless support experience for users working from different locations.

Example Scenario:

A user reports an issue with accessing a critical software application. The Help Desk Professional responds promptly, gathers relevant information about the error message, and utilizes the knowledge base to identify a potential solution. While troubleshooting, the professional maintains clear and empathetic communication, explaining the steps to the user. If the issue requires further investigation, the professional escalates it to the appropriate support tier and ensures the user is kept informed throughout the process. After resolution, the professional documents the steps taken, contributing valuable insights for future reference and continuous improvement.

These roles, responsibilities, and functions collectively enable Help Desk Professionals to provide efficient and effective support, contributing to the overall success of the organization

KEY Attributes, Traits and Qualities
of
Help Desk Professionals

1. Technical Proficiency:

Definition: A help desk professional should possess strong technical skills and a deep understanding of the products, services, or systems they are supporting.

Example: In an IT help desk role, proficiency in troubleshooting software and hardware issues, resolving network problems, and providing technical guidance to users.

2. Effective Communication:

Definition: Clear and concise communication is crucial for help desk professionals to understand user issues and convey solutions in a way that is easily understood.

Example: Articulating technical jargon in a user-friendly manner, actively listening to users' problems, and providing step-by-step instructions for issue resolution.

3. Patience and Empathy:

Definition: Help desk professionals should be patient when dealing with users who may not be tech-savvy and express empathy towards their frustrations.

Example: Remaining calm and understanding when assisting a user through a complex issue or patiently guiding someone unfamiliar with technology.

4. Problem-Solving Skills:

Definition: The ability to analyze problems, identify root causes, and develop effective solutions is a key attribute for help desk professionals.

Example: Diagnosing and resolving issues efficiently, troubleshooting errors, and finding innovative solutions to recurring problems.

5. Time Management:

Definition: Efficiently managing time is essential for handling multiple support tickets and ensuring timely responses to users' concerns.

Example: Prioritizing urgent issues, meeting service level agreements (SLAs), and effectively juggling multiple tasks without compromising quality.

6. Customer-Focused Mindset:

Definition: A customer-centric approach involves prioritizing the needs and satisfaction of users to ensure a positive experience.

Example: Going the extra mile to assist users, providing personalized support, and actively seeking feedback for continuous improvement.

7. Adaptability and Learning Agility:

Definition: Help desk professionals should be adaptable to evolving technologies and possess a willingness to continually learn and update their skills.

Example: Quickly adapting to new software updates, staying informed about emerging technologies, and proactively seeking training opportunities.

8. Analytical Thinking:

Definition: Help desk professionals need analytical skills to assess information, identify patterns, and make informed decisions.

Example: Analyzing system logs, identifying trends in support tickets to address root causes, and making data-driven decisions for process improvement.

9. Team Player:

Definition: Collaboration is often required in a help desk environment; professionals should work well within a team to share knowledge and collectively address challenges.

Example: Collaborating with colleagues to resolve complex issues, sharing insights, and contributing to team success.

10. Professionalism and Integrity:

Definition: Maintaining a high level of professionalism, integrity, and ethical behavior is essential for building trust with users.

Example: Handling sensitive user data with confidentiality, ensuring honesty in communication, and upholding ethical standards in all interactions.

11. Proactive Problem Prevention:

Definition: Help desk professionals should not only react to issues but also proactively identify potential problems and implement preventive measures.

Example: Monitoring system health, conducting regular maintenance checks, and implementing solutions to prevent recurring issues.

12. Strong Documentation Skills:

Definition: Thorough documentation is crucial for recording solutions, creating knowledge bases, and ensuring a smooth transition of information within the team.

Example: Documenting troubleshooting steps, resolutions, and common issues to create a comprehensive knowledge base for future reference.

Help desk professionals who embody these attributes contribute to a positive and efficient support environment, fostering user satisfaction and overall organizational success.

Telephone Techniques and Skills

In the digital age, where technology connects us instantaneously, mastering telephone techniques and skills is indispensable for effective customer service. This chapter delves into the intricacies of telephone communication, emphasizing the importance of the first contact, pre-call planning, handling calls with professionalism, and addressing complaints and angry customers.

The First Contact

Importance of Effective Telephone Communication

Effective telephone communication is a cornerstone of exceptional customer service. Unlike face-to-face interactions, telephone conversations rely solely on verbal cues, making the tone of voice, choice of words, and the ability to convey empathy paramount. Consider a scenario where a customer calls a helpline seeking assistance. A warm, reassuring voice and clear communication immediately set the stage for a positive interaction.

To illustrate, the success story of Ritz-Carlton stands out. Their telephone etiquette is legendary, and employees are trained to answer calls promptly, speak in a courteous tone, and actively listen to customers. This commitment to effective telephone communication has become a defining characteristic of the Ritz-Carlton brand.

Techniques for Building Rapport Over the Phone

Building rapport over the phone requires finesse and empathy. Simple techniques, such as using the customer's name, expressing genuine interest, and employing positive language, can go a long way.

Consider the example of Zane, a customer service representative known for building rapport. Zane not only addresses customer concerns but engages in friendly conversations, creating a personalized experience even in a virtual setting.

Key DO's & DON'T's in Professional Telephone Answering/ Receiving
Key DO's in Professional Telephone Answering for Help Desk Professionals:
  - ✓ Answer Promptly:
    Do: Answer calls promptly, ideally within the first few rings, to demonstrate responsiveness and efficiency.
  - ✓ Identify Yourself Clearly:
    Do: Clearly state your name, department, and organization when answering the phone to provide a professional introduction.
  - ✓ Active Listening:
    Do: Practice active listening to fully understand the caller's issue or inquiry. Repeat key points to ensure accuracy.
  - ✓ Speak Clearly and Professionally:
    Do: Speak in a clear, professional, and courteous manner. Avoid using slang or overly technical language that may confuse the caller.
  - ✓ Verify Caller's Information:
    Do: Verify the caller's identity, especially when handling sensitive information or providing access to account details.
  - ✓ Ask Open-Ended Questions:
    Do: Use open-ended questions to gather more information about the issue and guide the conversation toward a solution.

✓ Provide Estimated Resolution Time:
Do: Communicate an estimated resolution time if applicable, managing the caller's expectations regarding issue resolution.

✓ Offer Assistance Beyond the Immediate Issue:
Do: Offer additional assistance or information that may be relevant to the caller's needs, demonstrating a proactive approach.

✓ Use Positive Language:
Do: Use positive and reassuring language to convey confidence and competence in addressing the caller's concerns.

✓ Offer Clear Instructions:
Do: Provide clear and concise instructions, especially if the caller needs to perform certain actions to resolve their issue.

✓ Document the Call:
Do: Record essential details of the call, including the issue discussed, actions taken, and any promises made. This documentation is valuable for future reference.

✓ Follow Up as Promised:
Do: If follow-up is required, ensure you do so within the promised time frame. This builds trust and shows commitment to resolving issues.

Key DON'Ts in Professional Telephone Answering for Help Desk Professionals:

✓ Don't Interrupt the Caller:
Don't: Interrupt the caller while they are explaining their issue. Allow them to express their concerns fully before responding.

✓ Avoid Putting Callers on Prolonged Holds:

Don't: Keep callers on hold for extended periods without periodic updates. If necessary, inform them about the delay and offer alternatives.

✓ Avoid Negative Language:
Don't: Use negative language or expressions that may convey frustration or irritation. Maintain a positive and professional tone.

✓ Don't Guess Solutions:
Don't: Guess solutions if you are uncertain. Instead, acknowledge the uncertainty and assure the caller that you will investigate and provide accurate information.

✓ Avoid Jargon or Technical Terms:
Don't: Overuse technical jargon that may be confusing to non-technical callers. Explain technical terms in a clear and understandable manner.

✓ Don't Speak Too Quickly:
Don't: Speak too quickly, as it may make it challenging for the caller to follow instructions or understand information.

✓ Avoid Personal Conversations:
Don't: Engage in personal conversations or discussions unrelated to the caller's issue. Maintain a focus on professional communication.

✓ Don't Promise Unachievable Solutions:
Don't: Promise solutions that cannot be realistically delivered. Manage expectations and provide accurate information.

✓ Avoid Dismissive Attitudes:
Don't: Display a dismissive attitude toward the caller's concerns. Treat every inquiry with respect and importance.

✓ Don't Multitask During Calls:
   Don't: Multitask or engage in unrelated activities while on a call. Dedicate your full attention to the caller and their issue.
✓ Avoid Transferring Repeatedly:
   Don't: Transfer callers multiple times without attempting to resolve their issue first. Minimize unnecessary transfers to enhance the customer experience.
✓ Don't Forget to Summarize and Confirm:
   Don't: Forget to summarize the key points of the call before ending the conversation. Confirm that the caller is satisfied with the information provided or the actions taken.

Adhering to these DO's and DON'Ts ensures that help desk professionals provide a positive and effective telephone support experience for callers.

Pre-Call Planning and Preparation

Understanding the Customer's Background
Before answering a call, it is essential to gather relevant information about the customer. Understanding their history with the company, past interactions, and any ongoing issues allows the customer service representative to provide a more personalized and efficient service. For instance, a software support team may benefit from knowing the customer's prior technical challenges to streamline the troubleshooting process.

Anticipating Potential Issues
Anticipating potential issues is a proactive approach to problem-solving. By reviewing customer records and anticipating common challenges, customer service representatives can preemptively address concerns during the call. This strategy not only demonstrates foresight but also enhances the efficiency of the service call.

Steps that the HELP DESK Professionals must keep in mind when Preparing for a Call

Steps and Areas to Consider When Preparing for a Help Desk Call:
Self-Preparation:
- ✓ Understand Your Role: Clarify your role and responsibilities in the help desk. Know the extent of support you can provide.
- ✓ Review Training Materials: Refresh your knowledge by reviewing training materials, manuals, and any relevant documentation.

About the Customer:
- ✓ Review Customer Information: Check the customer's history and previous interactions. Understand their preferences and any ongoing issues.
- ✓ Anticipate Customer Needs: Based on past interactions, anticipate potential issues or questions the customer might have.

Market and Industry Knowledge:
- ✓ Stay Informed: Be aware of recent developments in the market or industry relevant to the products or services you support.
- ✓ Understanding Trends: Understand industry trends to provide context and additional insights during the call.

Tools and Software:
- ✓ Ensure Access to Tools: Make sure you have access to the necessary tools and software required to assist the customer.
- ✓ Update Knowledge on Tools: Stay updated on the features and updates of the tools you use for troubleshooting.

Documentation:
- ✓ Review Knowledge Base: Familiarize yourself with the knowledge base or documentation system. Ensure it's up to date with the latest information.
- ✓ Document Previous Interactions: If there are ongoing issues, review the documentation of previous interactions to provide a seamless experience for the customer.

Strategy and Approach:
- ✓ Define Call Objectives: Clearly define the objectives of the call. Know what you aim to achieve by the end of the conversation.
- ✓ Plan Troubleshooting Steps: Have a structured plan for troubleshooting common issues. This ensures a systematic approach to problem-solving.

Communication Skills:
- ✓ Practice Active Listening: Remind yourself of the importance of active listening. Ensure you give the customer your full attention.
- ✓ Use Clear and Concise Language: Practice using clear and concise language to convey information effectively.

Time Management:
- ✓ Prioritize Tasks: Prioritize tasks based on urgency and importance. Be mindful of time constraints during the call.
- ✓ Set Realistic Time Expectations: If further investigation is required, set realistic time expectations for the customer.

Customer Engagement:
- ✓ Build Rapport: Plan to build rapport with the customer. Establishing a positive connection can enhance the overall experience.
- ✓ Personalize Interaction: Use customer details to personalize the interaction. Acknowledge their history with the company.

Problem-Solving Mindset:
- ✓ Encourage Customer Involvement: Encourage the customer to actively participate in troubleshooting. This can lead to quicker issue resolution.

- ✓ Be Prepared for Complex Issues: Mentally prepare for complex issues and have escalation procedures in mind if required.

Review Previous Cases:
- ✓ Learn from Past Cases: If there were challenging cases in the past, review and learn from them. Apply lessons learned to improve future interactions.
- ✓ Identify Patterns: Identify recurring issues or patterns in previous cases to address root causes.

Stay Calm and Composed:
- ✓ Practice Stress Management: Remind yourself to stay calm under pressure. Stress management is crucial for effective problem-solving.
- ✓ Take Breaks If Needed: If the workload is intense, plan for short breaks to recharge and maintain focus.

By considering these steps and areas before a help desk call, professionals can ensure they are well-prepared to provide efficient and effective support to customers. Preparedness contributes to a positive customer experience and helps build trust and confidence in the help desk's capabilities.

During the Call: Steps to a Professional Service Call

Addressing Customer Issues with Professionalism

During the call, addressing customer issues with professionalism is paramount. This involves active listening, acknowledging concerns, and providing clear and concise solutions. Imagine a scenario where a customer calls a technical support hotline with a complex issue. The professional service call hinges on the representative's ability to navigate the problem calmly, ensuring the customer feels heard and valued.

Factors to Consider During a Help Desk Call:

Active Listening:

- ✓ Focus on the Caller: Give your full attention to the caller. Avoid distractions and actively listen to understand their concerns.
- ✓ Example: "I appreciate you bringing this to my attention. Can you please provide more details so I can better assist you?"

Clarification of Issues:

- ✓ Ask Clarifying Questions: Seek clarification on any ambiguous information provided by the caller to ensure a complete understanding of the issue.
- ✓ Example: "Could you please elaborate on the error message you're seeing? This will help me pinpoint the issue more accurately."

Empathy and Understanding:

- ✓ Express Empathy: Acknowledge the frustration or inconvenience the customer may be experiencing and convey understanding.
- ✓ Example: "I understand that dealing with technical issues can be frustrating. I'm here to help and will do my best to resolve this for you."

Effective Communication:

- ✓ Use Clear and Concise Language: Communicate solutions and instructions in a clear and straightforward manner, avoiding technical jargon.
- ✓ Example: "Let me guide you through the steps to resolve this issue. It's a simple process that should take a few minutes."

Provide Timely Updates:

- ✓ Keep the Caller Informed: If additional time is needed for troubleshooting, inform the caller and provide estimated completion times.
- ✓ Example: "I appreciate your patience. I'm still working on this, and I'll provide you with an update in the next couple of minutes."

Confirmation of Understanding:

- ✓ Ensure Caller Comprehension: Confirm that the caller understands any instructions or information provided during the call.
- ✓ Example: "Before we proceed, could you please confirm that you understand the steps we discussed?"

Resolution Progress:

- ✓ Update on Progress: Provide periodic updates on the progress of issue resolution, keeping the caller informed.

- Example: "I've identified the root cause and am implementing a solution. I'll let you know once it's resolved."

Customer Collaboration:
- ✓ Encourage Customer Participation: Involve the customer in the troubleshooting process, especially if actions need to be taken on their end.
- ✓ Example: "To better understand the issue, could you perform a quick check on your end and let me know the results?"

Calm and Professional Demeanor:
- ✓ Maintain Professionalism: Stay calm and professional, even in challenging situations. This fosters a positive customer experience.
- ✓ Example: "I appreciate your cooperation. We're working together to resolve this issue, and I'm committed to finding a solution for you."

Flexibility in Approach:
- ✓ Adapt to Changing Situations: Be flexible and adapt your approach based on the evolving nature of the call.
- ✓ Example: "It seems we've encountered an unexpected issue. Let me adjust our approach to address this effectively."

Knowledge Utilization:
- ✓ Apply Technical Knowledge: Utilize your technical knowledge and expertise to efficiently troubleshoot and resolve issues.
- ✓ Example: "Based on the symptoms you've described, I suspect this could be related to a known issue. Let's explore that possibility."

Closure and Confirmation:

- ✓ Confirm Issue Resolution: Before concluding the call, confirm with the caller that the issue has been resolved to their satisfaction.
- ✓ Example: "It looks like the issue is resolved now. Is everything working as expected on your end?"

By considering these steps and areas during a help desk call, professionals can enhance their ability to effectively address customer concerns, provide timely and clear communication, and ultimately contribute to a positive customer experience.

Effective Questioning and Listening Skills

Effective questioning and listening skills are fundamental to understanding customer needs. Open-ended questions encourage customers to share more information, while attentive listening ensures a comprehensive understanding of their concerns. Consider the case of Amazon's customer service, where representatives are trained to ask probing questions to identify root issues and provide tailored solutions.

Examples of Questions that Help Desk Personnel can Ask to Uncover Issues

Here are some examples of questions that a help desk professional can ask to uncover and understand the issues:

- ✓ General Issue Identification:
  Example: "Could you please describe the specific problem or error message you're encountering?"
  Example: "When did you first notice this issue, and has it happened consistently since then?"
- ✓ Environment and Setup:
  Example: "Can you tell me about the devices or systems you are currently using?"
  Example: "Have there been any recent changes to your system or network configuration?"
- ✓ User Actions and Patterns:
  Example: "Can you walk me through the steps you took before encountering the issue?"

Example: "Does the problem occur consistently, or does it seem to happen under specific circumstances?"

✓ Error Messages or Codes:
Example: "Are you receiving any error messages on your screen? If so, could you provide the exact text?"
Example: "Have you noted any error codes associated with the issue?"

✓ Frequency and Occurrence:
Example: "How often does this problem occur? Is it a constant issue, or does it happen intermittently?"
Example: "Have you noticed any patterns regarding the time of day or specific activities when the issue arises?"

✓ Recent Changes or Updates:
Example: "Have there been any recent software updates or installations on your system?"
Example: "Did you make any changes to your configuration or settings before experiencing the problem?"

✓ Browser or Application Specifics:
Example: "Are you experiencing this issue in a specific browser or application?"
Example: "Have you tried accessing the same content using a different browser or application?"

✓ User Permissions and Access:
Example: "Do you have the necessary permissions to access the features or data causing the issue?"
Example: "Have there been any changes to your user account or access privileges?"

✓ Network Connectivity:
Example: "Is your internet connection stable, or have you experienced any disruptions recently?"
Example: "Have you tested the issue on different networks to see if the problem persists?"
✓ Hardware Checks:
Example: "Have you performed any hardware checks, such as ensuring all cables are securely connected?"
Example: "Are there any unusual noises or behaviors from your hardware that you've observed?"
✓ Previous Issue Resolutions:
Example: "Have you encountered a similar problem in the past, and if so, how was it resolved?"
Example: "Were there any temporary solutions you applied that may give insight into the issue?"
✓ User Skill Level:
Example: "Could you share your level of familiarity with the system or software you're using?"
Example: "Are there specific features or functionalities you find challenging to navigate?"
✓ Collaboration with Other Users:
Example: "Have you checked with colleagues or peers to see if they are experiencing a similar problem?"
Example: "Is this issue affecting multiple users or just your account?"
✓ Security and Privacy Concerns:

Example: "Have you noticed any unusual activities or potential security threats before the issue occurred?"
Example: "Can you confirm that your antivirus software is up to date and running scans regularly?"

✓ End-User Expectations:
Example: "What outcome or resolution are you expecting from our assistance today?"
Example: "Is there a specific goal or task you are trying to achieve, and the issue is hindering that process?"

These questions are designed to gather detailed information, enabling help desk professionals to diagnose and address issues more effectively.

Open-ended Questions to get to the Root of Issues in Various Categories of Industries

Open-ended questions are instrumental in uncovering detailed information and getting to the root of issues. Below are examples of 10 open questions tailored for different categories of industries or service providers. These questions aim to facilitate a deeper understanding of specific challenges users might face:

1. Information Technology (IT) Industry:

Software Issues:
- ✓ "Can you describe in detail what happens when you encounter the error message?"
- ✓ "Have there been any recent software updates or changes to your system configuration?"
- ✓ "What specific actions were you performing when the issue occurred?"
- ✓ "Are other users in your department experiencing similar problems?"
- ✓ "Can you walk me through the steps you took leading up to the problem?"

Hardware Troubleshooting:
- ✓ "When did you first notice the hardware issue, and under what circumstances?"
- ✓ "Have there been any recent physical changes to your workstation or device?"
- ✓ "Can you provide details on any unusual sounds or signs before the hardware problem?"
- ✓ "Are there specific applications or tasks that seem to trigger the hardware issue?"

✓ "How often does the hardware problem occur, and is it intermittent or consistent?"

Network Connectivity:
- ✓ "Are you experiencing network issues on a wired or wireless connection?"
- ✓ "Can you identify specific websites or applications affected by the connectivity problem?"
- ✓ "Have there been recent changes to your network configuration or equipment?"
- ✓ "Are other devices in your vicinity experiencing similar network disruptions?"
- ✓ "Can you perform a speed test and share the results to help diagnose the issue?"

2. Healthcare Industry:

Electronic Health Record (EHR) Access:
- ✓ "Can you provide details about the specific patient records or sections you're having trouble accessing?"
- ✓ "Are there any error messages or prompts that appear when trying to access the EHR?"
- ✓ "Have there been recent updates or changes to the EHR system?"
- ✓ "Are other healthcare providers experiencing similar difficulties with EHR access?"
- ✓ "Can you describe any patterns or trends regarding when the access issue occurs?"

Medical Equipment Malfunctions:
- ✓ "Which specific medical equipment is displaying issues, and what functions are affected?"
- ✓ "Can you recall any unusual sounds or behaviors from the equipment before the malfunction?"

✓ "Has routine maintenance or calibration been performed on the equipment recently?"
✓ "Are other healthcare professionals reporting similar malfunctions with the equipment?"
✓ "Can you identify any specific patient scenarios associated with the equipment issues?"

3. Financial Services Industry:
Online Banking or Transactions:
✓ "What specific steps are you taking when encountering issues with online banking transactions?"
✓ "Have there been recent updates to your online banking or changes in account details?"
✓ "Are the issues occurring consistently, or is there a specific time or transaction type affected?"
✓ "Have you received any error messages or alerts during the online banking process?"
✓ "Can you provide details on the types of transactions affected by the issue?"

Credit Card Processing:
✓ "Which specific credit card transactions are experiencing difficulties, and at what point in the process?"
✓ "Have there been recent changes to the credit card processing system or merchant account?"
✓ "Can you describe any error messages or decline codes received during the processing?"
✓ "Are other merchants within your network reporting similar credit card processing issues?"

- ✓ "Can you identify any patterns related to specific card types or issuing banks?"

4. Education Sector:
Learning Management System (LMS) Issues:
- ✓ "When do you typically encounter problems with the LMS, and is it related to specific activities?"
- ✓ "Have there been recent updates or changes to the LMS system?"
- ✓ "Can you describe any error messages or issues you see while navigating the LMS?"
- ✓ "Are other educators or students experiencing similar difficulties with the LMS?"
- ✓ "Can you identify specific courses or modules affected by the LMS issues?"

Classroom Technology:
- ✓ "Which specific classroom technologies are causing disruptions, and when do these disruptions occur?"
- ✓ "Have there been recent changes or updates to the classroom technology setup?"
- ✓ "Can you provide details on any error messages or malfunctions observed with the technology?"
- ✓ "Are other educators experiencing similar challenges with classroom technology?"
- ✓ "Can you recall any patterns or trends related to the timing or frequency of technology issues?"

5. Retail Industry:
Point of Sale (POS) System Problems:
- ✓ "What specific actions are you taking when encountering issues with the POS system?"
- ✓ "Have there been recent updates or changes to the POS software or hardware?"

- ✓ "Can you describe any error messages or issues during the transaction process?"
- ✓ "Are other employees or branches reporting similar challenges with the POS system?"
- ✓ "Can you identify any patterns related to the type of transactions affected or time of day?"

These open-ended questions are designed to encourage users to provide detailed information, enabling Help Desk Professionals to diagnose and resolve issues more effectively across various industry sectors. Adjust the questions based on the specific context and nuances of the organization or industry.

Steps to be a Good Listener

Being a good listener is crucial for help desk professionals to understand and address customer issues effectively. Here are steps they can take along with examples:

1. **Give Full Attention:**
   Example: When on a call, avoid multitasking or distractions. Focus solely on the customer's voice and the details they are providing.

2. **Avoid Interrupting:**
   Example: Let the customer express their concerns fully without interruptions. Only interject when they've finished sharing their thoughts.

3. **Use Positive Non-Verbal Cues:**
   Example: Nodding, using affirming facial expressions, and providing verbal cues like *"I understand"* convey active engagement and encouragement.

4. **Paraphrase to Confirm Understanding:**
   Example: Repeat back key points the customer has shared to confirm your understanding. *"So, if I understand correctly, the issue started after the recent software update."*

5. **Ask Clarifying Questions:**
   Example: Seek clarification when details are unclear. *"Could you please provide more information about the specific error message you encountered?"*

6. **Empathize with the Customer:**

Example: Express empathy to show understanding of the customer's frustration. *"I can imagine how challenging it must be to deal with this issue."*

7. **Summarize Key Points:**
   Example: Periodically summarize the information the customer has provided to ensure accuracy. *"Let me summarize what we've discussed so far to make sure I have all the details."*

8. **Avoid Prejudgments:**
   Example: Avoid making assumptions or forming conclusions before the customer has finished explaining their issue. *"I want to make sure I understand the situation fully, so please share all the details."*

9. **Reflect Feelings:**
   Example: Acknowledge the customer's emotions and reflect them back. *"It sounds like you're frustrated with the recurring issues you've been facing."*

10. **Use Open-Ended Questions:**
    Example: Encourage detailed responses by asking open-ended questions. *"Can you share more about the circumstances leading up to the problem?"*

11. **Clarify Customer Expectations:**
    Example: Ensure a mutual understanding of expectations by asking, *"What outcome are you hoping for, and how can I best assist you?"*

12. **Remain Silent When Needed:**
    Example: Allow brief pauses to give the customer time to gather their thoughts or share additional details without feeling rushed.

13. **Show Genuine Interest:**
    Example: Express genuine curiosity about the customer's experience. *"I'm interested in learning more about your perspective. Can you provide more context?"*
14. **Focus on the Message, Not Delivery:**
    Example: Pay attention to the substance of the customer's message rather than critiquing their communication style or tone.
15. **Provide Regular Feedback:**
    Example: Confirm your active listening by offering feedback. *"Thank you for sharing that information. I want to assure you that I'm actively working on resolving the issue."*
16. **Record Key Details:**
    Example: Take notes during the conversation to capture essential details that may aid in problem resolution or future reference.
17. **Follow-Up Questions:**
    Example: Ask follow-up questions to delve deeper into specific aspects of the customer's issue. *"Can you provide more details about what happened just before the problem occurred?"*

By incorporating these steps and examples into their communication style, help desk professionals can enhance their listening skills, fostering better understanding, and improving overall customer satisfaction.

Handling Complaints and Angry Customers

Encouraging Complaints as Opportunities for Improvement

Complaints, when handled adeptly, can be opportunities for improvement. Encouraging customers to voice concerns not only defuses tension but also provides valuable insights into areas that may need enhancement. An example is the online retailer Zappos, where customer service representatives actively encourage customers to share feedback, turning potential complaints into opportunities for continuous improvement.

Step by Step Action Plan along to Handle Angry/ Irate Customers

Handling angry or irate customers requires a delicate and empathetic approach. Here's a step-by-step action plan with examples:

Step 1: Stay Calm and Composed

Example: Take a deep breath before responding. Maintain a calm and composed demeanor, even if the customer is expressing frustration.

Step 2: Listen Actively

Example: Allow the customer to vent without interruption. *"I'm here to listen. Please share your concerns, and I'll do my best to assist you."*

Step 3: Empathize with the Customer

Example: Express understanding of their frustration. *"I can hear that you're upset, and I genuinely apologize for any inconvenience you've experienced."*

Step 4: Use Positive Language

Example: Reframe negative statements positively. Instead of saying "*I can't do that,*" say "*Let me find a solution that works for both of us.*"

Step 5: Apologize Sincerely

Example: *"I apologize for any inconvenience or frustration you've encountered. I understand this is important, and we want to make it right."*

Step 6: Acknowledge the Issue

Example: Acknowledge their specific concerns. *"I understand that the delayed delivery has caused inconvenience, and I'm here to address it."*

Step 7: Avoid Blame

Example: Refrain from placing blame. Instead, focus on resolving the issue. *"I appreciate you bringing this to our attention. Let's work together to find a solution."*

Step 8: Offer a Solution or Next Steps

Example: *"To address this, I can [propose a solution or action]. Does that sound acceptable to you?"*

Step 9: Set Realistic Expectations

Example: Be transparent about the resolution timeframe. *"I'll prioritize this and provide you with an update within [specified timeframe]."*

Step 10: Seek Confirmation

Example: *"Does the proposed solution align with your expectations? Is there anything else you'd like me to consider in resolving this matter?"*

Step 11: Follow Up

Example: After implementing the solution, follow up to ensure satisfaction. *"I wanted to check in to see if the solution resolved the issue to your satisfaction."*

Step 12: Document the Interaction

Example: Record details of the conversation for reference and to ensure a consistent approach in future interactions.

Step 13: Report to Management (if needed)
Example: If the issue requires escalation, communicate the details to the appropriate channels for further investigation and resolution.
Step 14: Implement Preventive Measures
Example: If the issue is recurring, explore preventive measures and share them with the customer. *"To avoid similar issues in the future, here are some steps we can take..."*
Step 15: Express Gratitude
Example: *"I appreciate your patience and understanding in resolving this matter. If you have any further concerns, please don't hesitate to reach out."*

By following this step-by-step action plan, help desk professionals can effectively manage and defuse situations involving angry or irate customers, turning negative experiences into opportunities for positive resolution and customer satisfaction.

Resolving Complaints Effectively

Step by Step Action Plan to Resolve Complaints
Resolving complaints involves a systematic approach that focuses on understanding the issue, addressing it effectively, and ensuring customer satisfaction.

Here's a step-by-step action plan with examples:
Step 1: Acknowledge the Complaint
Example: *"Thank you for bringing this to our attention. I'm sorry to hear about the issue you're facing. Let's work together to resolve it."*
Step 2: Express Empathy
Example: *"I understand that dealing with this problem has been frustrating. I genuinely apologize for any inconvenience caused."*
Step 3: Listen Actively
Example: *"Please share the details of the complaint. I'm here to listen and understand the situation fully."*
Step 4: Ask Clarifying Questions
Example: *"To better assist you, could you provide more details or clarify certain aspects of the issue you're experiencing?"*
Step 5: Apologize Sincerely
Example: *"I want to sincerely apologize for any inconvenience this has caused you. We appreciate your patience as we work to resolve this."*
Step 6: Investigate the Issue
Example: *"Let me look into the matter and gather more information to understand the root cause. This will help us find a lasting solution."*
Step 7: Provide Regular Updates

Example: *"I'll keep you updated on our progress. In the meantime, is there a preferred method of communication for updates?"*

Step 8: Propose a Solution

Example: *"Based on our investigation, here's a proposed solution. Does this align with your expectations, or is there something else you'd prefer?"*

Step 9: Implement the Solution

Example: *"I'll initiate the necessary steps to implement the solution. Please let me know if you have any specific concerns or preferences."*

Step 10: Follow Up

Example: After the solution is implemented, follow up with the customer to ensure satisfaction. *"I wanted to check if the solution resolved the issue to your satisfaction."*

Step 11: Seek Feedback

Example: *"Your feedback is valuable to us. Is there anything we could have done differently, or any additional support you might need?"*

Step 12: Document the Resolution

Example: Record details of the resolution, including the steps taken and the customer's feedback, for future reference and improvement.

Step 13: Implement Preventive Measures

Example: *"To prevent similar issues in the future, we'll be implementing [preventive measures]. This will enhance our service quality moving forward."*

Step 14: Express Gratitude

Example: *"Thank you for bringing this to our attention, and for your patience throughout the resolution process. We value your feedback and strive to continually improve."*

Step 15: Continuous Improvement

Example: *"We're committed to learning from this experience and improving our processes to ensure a better experience for you and all our customers."*

By following this step-by-step action plan, help desk professionals can effectively handle and resolve complaints, demonstrating responsiveness, empathy, and a commitment to customer satisfaction.

Empowering Frontline Staff to Resolve Issues

Empowering frontline staff to resolve issues is a strategic approach to efficient complaint resolution. By providing training, clear guidelines, and the authority to make decisions, companies enable their frontline staff to address complaints promptly. A case in point is the hospitality industry, where front desk staff in hotels are often empowered to resolve customer issues on the spot, fostering a sense of immediacy and customer satisfaction.

Various ways by which organizations can Empower Frontline Staff to Resolve Issues

Empowering frontline staff to resolve issues is essential for providing efficient and effective customer service. Here are various ways organizations can achieve this:

- ✓ Comprehensive Training Programs:
  Example: Provide thorough training on product knowledge, customer service skills, and problem-solving techniques to ensure frontline staff is well-equipped to handle a variety of issues.
- ✓ Clear Communication Channels:
  Example: Establish open communication channels between frontline staff and management to ensure a seamless flow of information. Regular updates on policies and procedures are crucial.
- ✓ Delegate Decision-Making Authority:
  Example: Empower frontline staff by allowing them to make certain decisions without

constant supervision. This fosters a sense of responsibility and autonomy.
- ✓ Use of Decision Trees and Guidelines:
Example: Provide decision-making frameworks and guidelines that frontline staff can reference when dealing with common issues. Decision trees can help streamline the process.
- ✓ Regular Feedback and Coaching:
Example: Implement regular feedback sessions and coaching programs to provide constructive input and guidance for improvement. Recognize and celebrate successful issue resolutions.
- ✓ Encourage Creativity and Innovation:
Example: Foster a culture that encourages frontline staff to think creatively and propose innovative solutions to common problems. Recognize and reward innovative problem-solving.
- ✓ Access to Resources and Tools:
Example: Ensure that frontline staff have easy access to relevant resources, knowledge bases, and tools that can aid in issue resolution, reducing dependency on higher authorities.
- ✓ Cross-Training Opportunities:
Example: Provide cross-training opportunities so that frontline staff can gain exposure to different aspects of the organization, making them more versatile in resolving a variety of issues.
- ✓ Real-Time Decision Support Systems:
Example: Implement real-time decision support systems that offer guidance and

suggestions to frontline staff as they handle customer issues, ensuring consistent and accurate resolutions.

✓ Encourage Collaborative Problem-Solving:
Example: Create a culture of collaboration where frontline staff can share insights and solutions with their peers. This collective knowledge-sharing enhances the overall problem-solving capability of the team.

✓ Empowerment through Technology:
Example: Invest in technology that allows frontline staff to access customer information, historical data, and relevant resources swiftly, enabling them to resolve issues more efficiently.

✓ Customer Feedback Integration:
Example: Integrate customer feedback into the resolution process. Use customer insights to identify areas for improvement and recognize successful issue resolutions.

✓ Recognition and Rewards:
Example: Establish a recognition program that acknowledges frontline staff for exceptional issue resolution. Rewards, whether monetary or through public recognition, can motivate staff.

✓ Empathy Training:
Example: Provide training on empathy and emotional intelligence, enabling frontline staff to understand and connect with customers, leading to more effective issue resolution.

✓ Define Clear Service Standards:
Example: Clearly define service standards and expectations, empowering frontline staff with a

set of guidelines that align with the organization's values and goals.
✓ Continuous Improvement Culture:
Example: Foster a culture of continuous improvement where frontline staff actively participate in identifying areas for improvement and contribute ideas for better issue resolution processes.

By implementing these strategies, organizations can empower their frontline staff to take ownership of issue resolution, leading to enhanced customer satisfaction and a more efficient customer service process.

Personal (Face to Face) Interaction

In the realm of customer service, face-to-face interactions hold a unique significance. This chapter explores the nuances of personal interaction, delving into the importance of enhancing personal qualities and the essential customer care skills required for fostering positive relationships.

Enhancing Personal Qualities
Creating and Presenting a Professional Image
Creating and presenting a professional image is the first step in personal interaction. It's about more than just appearance; it encompasses the entire package that a customer sees, hears, and experiences. Take, for example, the luxury retail sector. Sales associates in high-end boutiques not only dress impeccably but also exude an air of sophistication and knowledge about their products. This professional image contributes to the overall perception of the brand and influences the customer's trust and confidence.
Action Plan: Implement a dress code and grooming policy that aligns with your company's brand identity. Conduct regular training sessions to emphasize the importance of professional demeanor, including posture, tone of voice, and overall presentation.
Personal Grooming for Customer Care
Personal grooming extends beyond attire. It includes grooming in communication, behavior, and interpersonal skills. Imagine a scenario where a customer visits a spa for a relaxing massage. The receptionist's ability to communicate effectively, offer a warm greeting, and maintain a positive attitude contributes to the overall customer experience.

Personal grooming in this context involves training staff to embody the values of the business and convey them through their interactions.

Action Plan: Develop training programs focused on effective communication, empathy, and interpersonal skills. Encourage staff to actively engage in continuous self-improvement, ensuring that they are well-equipped to provide a positive and memorable experience for customers.

Ensuring Proper Grooming and Presenting a Professional Image

Ensuring proper grooming and presenting a professional image is crucial for help desk personnel, as it contributes to creating a positive first impression. Here are various steps they can take along with examples:

1. Personal Hygiene:
- ✓ Explanation: Maintain good personal hygiene by regularly showering, brushing teeth, and wearing clean, pressed clothing.
- ✓ Example: A help desk professional should ensure they are well-groomed, with clean and neatly styled hair, fresh breath, and an overall tidy appearance.

2. Appropriate Attire:
- ✓ Explanation: Dress in accordance with the company's dress code, choosing professional and clean attire.
- ✓ Example: For a corporate setting, this might involve wearing business casual or formal attire, avoiding overly casual or revealing clothing.

3. Neat and Tidy Workspace:
- ✓ Explanation: Maintain a clean and organized workspace, as it reflects professionalism and attention to detail.
- ✓ Example: Keep the desk clutter-free, organize cables, and ensure all necessary tools and resources are readily accessible.

4. Professional Accessories:

✓ Explanation: Choose accessories that enhance a professional image, such as a simple watch or minimal jewelry.

✓ Example: Wearing a watch that complements the outfit can add a touch of sophistication without being overly flashy.

5. Confidence in Posture:

✓ Explanation: Maintain good posture to convey confidence and professionalism.

✓ Example: Stand or sit up straight, avoiding slouching, to project an image of attentiveness and competence.

6. Cultural Sensitivity:

✓ Explanation: Be mindful of cultural norms and sensitivities when it comes to grooming choices and attire.

✓ Example: Some cultures may have specific expectations regarding dress and appearance, and it's important to respect and adhere to these norms.

7. Effective Communication Skills:

✓ Explanation: Communicate clearly and professionally, both verbally and non-verbally.

✓ Example: Use polite language, maintain eye contact, and be attentive when listening to customers' concerns.

8. Minimal Use of Fragrances:

✓ Explanation: Avoid excessive use of perfumes or colognes, as strong scents may be distracting or unpleasant for others.

✓ Example: Opt for subtle fragrances or skip them altogether to maintain a professional and considerate environment.

9. Appropriate Use of Makeup:

✓ Explanation: If makeup is worn, keep it subtle and professional.

✓ Example: Choose natural tones for makeup that enhance rather than distract from a professional appearance.

10. Well-Maintained Footwear:

✓ Explanation: Ensure footwear is clean, polished, and appropriate for the workplace.

✓ Example: In a business casual setting, polished loafers or dress shoes would be suitable, while sneakers might be appropriate in more casual environments.

11. Hair care and Hairstyle:

✓ Explanation: Keep hair well-groomed and styled in a manner that aligns with the company's expectations.

✓ Example: A neat hairstyle that is well-maintained reflects attention to personal grooming.

12. Time Management:

✓ Explanation: Arrive punctually for work and appointments, demonstrating reliability.

✓ Example: Being on time for shifts and meetings shows a commitment to professionalism and respect for others' time.

13. Adaptability to Dress Codes:

✓ Explanation: Adapt grooming and attire based on the formality of the workplace or specific events.

✓ Example: .Attending a formal meeting may require a suit, while a casual Friday might permit more relaxed attire within the dress code.

14. Continual Professional Development:

✓ Explanation: Stay informed about any updates or changes in the company's dress code or grooming expectations.
✓ Example: Attend training sessions or read company policies to ensure ongoing compliance with grooming standards.

15. Positive Body Language:
✓ Explanation: Display positive body language, including smiling, maintaining eye contact, and offering a firm handshake.
✓ Example: A friendly and open demeanor contributes to a welcoming and professional image.

By following these steps, help desk personnel can ensure they present a polished and professional image, creating a positive impression on customers and colleagues alike.

Customer Care Skills

Viewing Complaints as Gifts

Customer care skills go beyond the transactional aspects of a service encounter; they involve cultivating a mindset that views complaints as opportunities for improvement. Consider the hospitality sector, where renowned hotels often receive detailed feedback from guests. The ability to view complaints as gifts allows these establishments to continuously refine their services, leading to elevated customer satisfaction and loyalty.

Action Plan: Implement a feedback system that encourages customers to provide constructive criticism. Train staff to perceive complaints positively, focusing on solutions and improvements rather than seeing them as setbacks.

Understanding the Current Complaints Culture in the Organization

Every organization has its unique complaints culture. This involves the processes, channels, and attitudes towards addressing customer concerns. Understanding this culture is critical for effective complaint resolution. For instance, in the tech industry, where products may undergo frequent updates, understanding the customer's perspective on changes helps in tailoring support and minimizing dissatisfaction.

Action Plan: Conduct a thorough analysis of the current complaints culture within the organization. Identify bottlenecks, gaps, and areas of improvement. Develop streamlined processes and communication channels to enhance the overall complaint resolution experience.

Complaints Culture Assessment Template

Objective: *Evaluate and analyze the current complaints culture within the organization, identify bottlenecks, gaps, and areas for improvement. Develop streamlined processes and communication channels to enhance the overall complaint resolution experience.*

1. Introduction:
- ✓ Purpose: Understand the existing complaints culture and identify opportunities for improvement.
- ✓ Scope: Assess the entire complaint resolution process and associated communication channels.

2. Current Complaints Culture Analysis:

Overview:
- ✓ Analyze the overall volume and nature of complaints.
- ✓ Identify the most common types of issues raised by customers.

Data Collection:
- ✓ Review historical complaint data.
- ✓ Evaluate the effectiveness of the current data collection methods.

Feedback Channels:
- ✓ Assess the accessibility and effectiveness of current feedback channels.
- ✓ Identify if feedback channels cover all customer touchpoints.

3. Bottlenecks and Gaps Identification:

Process Bottlenecks:
- ✓ Identify any delays or bottlenecks in the complaint resolution process.

✓ Examine whether there are specific stages where complaints tend to get stuck.

Communication Gaps:

✓ Evaluate the communication flow between customers, frontline staff, and management.

✓ Identify gaps in communication that may hinder effective complaint resolution.

4. Root Cause Analysis:

Root Causes of Complaints:

✓ Conduct a thorough analysis to identify the root causes of recurring complaints.

✓ Determine whether issues are systemic or isolated incidents.

Employee Feedback:

✓ Gather feedback from frontline staff on challenges faced during complaint resolution.

✓ Identify any obstacles preventing staff from resolving complaints efficiently.

5. Customer Experience Evaluation:

✓ Customer Journey Mapping:

✓ Map the customer journey during the complaint resolution process.

✓ Assess touchpoints and identify pain points from the customer's perspective.

Customer Satisfaction Surveys:

✓ Analyze results from customer satisfaction surveys related to complaint resolution.

✓ Identify areas where customer expectations are not being met.

6. Streamlined Processes and Communication Channels:

Process Redesign:

✓ Propose changes to the complaint resolution process to eliminate bottlenecks.

✓ Introduce efficiency measures to streamline the overall process.

Communication Enhancement:
- ✓ Introduce or improve communication channels for customers to submit and track complaints.
- ✓ Implement regular updates to keep customers informed of the resolution status.

7. Employee Training and Development:

Training Needs Analysis:
- ✓ Assess the need for additional training on complaint resolution for frontline staff.
- ✓ Identify specific skills or knowledge gaps.

Continuous Improvement Culture:
- ✓ Promote a culture of continuous improvement among staff.
- ✓ Encourage feedback from employees on ways to enhance the complaint resolution process.

8. Technology Integration:

Implement Technology Solutions:
- ✓ Explore technological tools that can automate and streamline the complaint resolution process.
- ✓ Integrate systems for better data management and reporting.

9. Performance Metrics and KPIs:

Define Key Metrics:
- ✓ Establish key performance indicators (KPIs) for measuring complaint resolution success.
- ✓ Develop metrics that align with organizational goals and customer satisfaction.

10. Implementation Plan:

Action Items:
- ✓ Clearly outline actionable steps based on the assessment findings.

✓ Assign responsibilities to relevant stakeholders for each action item.

Timeline:
- ✓ Develop a realistic timeline for the implementation of proposed changes.
- ✓ Set milestones for tracking progress.

11. Monitoring and Evaluation:

Monitoring Mechanism:
- ✓ Establish a monitoring system to track the effectiveness of implemented changes.
- ✓ Regularly review complaint resolution data and adjust strategies accordingly.

Continuous Feedback Loop:
- ✓ Implement a continuous feedback loop for both customers and employees to provide ongoing insights for improvement.

12. Reporting and Documentation:

Reporting Structure:
- ✓ Define a reporting structure for ongoing evaluation of the complaints culture.
- ✓ Establish regular reporting mechanisms to communicate progress to relevant stakeholders.

13. Conclusion:

Summary:
- ✓ Summarize the key findings of the assessment.
- ✓ Emphasize the potential impact of proposed changes on the overall complaints culture.

14. Appendix:
- ✓ Attach supporting documents, survey results, and additional data used in the assessment.

This comprehensive template provides a structured approach to assessing the current complaints culture, identifying areas for improvement, and developing a strategic plan for enhancing the overall complaint resolution experience within the organization.

Internet Interaction (Email)

In an era dominated by digital communication, mastering internet interaction, particularly through email, is a critical facet of providing excellent customer service. This chapter explores the nuances of email communication, delving into the importance of written communication etiquette, the timeliness of responses, and the strategic implementation of customer-defined standards.

Importance of Email Communication

Written Communication Etiquette

Emails are a direct representation of a company's professionalism and attention to detail. Written communication etiquette in email interactions is paramount. Consider a scenario where a customer reaches out to an e-commerce company with a product query. A prompt, well-crafted response not only addresses the customer's concerns but also reflects positively on the company's brand image.

Action Plan: Develop a set of written communication guidelines for email interactions. Emphasize clarity, professionalism, and a customer-friendly tone. Conduct training sessions to ensure all staff members are well-versed in these guidelines.

Timely and Effective Responses

The speed of response in email communication is a crucial factor influencing customer satisfaction. In today's fast-paced digital environment, customers expect timely and effective responses. For instance, a customer submitting a support ticket expects acknowledgment and initial guidance promptly. Delays can lead to frustration and a negative perception of the company.

Action Plan: Implement a response time policy for email interactions. Set realistic expectations for response times and ensure that staff members are equipped to meet these deadlines. Utilize automated acknowledgment systems for immediate response, even if a comprehensive resolution takes longer.

Creating Customer-Defined Standards

Measuring Success in Email Interactions

To create customer-defined standards, it is imperative to measure success in email interactions. This involves tracking key performance indicators (KPIs) such as response time, customer satisfaction scores, and issue resolution rates. Analyzing these metrics provides insights into the effectiveness of email communication and areas that may require improvement.

Action Plan: Implement a robust system for measuring success in email interactions. Utilize customer feedback, conduct regular surveys, and analyze response times. Identify patterns and trends to understand the strengths and weaknesses of current practices.

Using Measurement Results for Continuous Improvement

Measurement results become valuable tools for continuous improvement. Once data is collected, it should be used strategically to refine processes, enhance communication skills, and optimize the overall customer experience. A practical example is an online streaming service that tracks user feedback on email responses. By identifying common concerns and addressing them proactively, the service enhances user satisfaction and loyalty.

Action Plan: Establish a feedback loop where measurement results inform ongoing training programs and process improvements. Encourage a culture of continuous learning, where staff members are empowered to adapt and evolve based on the insights derived from measurement data.

Professional DO's & DON'T's of Emailing

Email Etiquette for Help Desk Personnel: DO's and DON'Ts
DO's:

Use a Professional Email Address:
- ✓ Do: Use a professional email address associated with the organization.
- ✓ Example: Gerard.Assey@Company.com

Clear and Concise Subject Lines:
- ✓ Do: Create subject lines that clearly convey the purpose of the email.
- ✓ Example: Subject: Request for Password Reset

Greet and Address Properly:
- ✓ Do: Start with a polite greeting and address the recipient appropriately.
- ✓ Example: Dear [Customer's Name],

Be Clear and Concise:
- ✓ Do: Clearly articulate your message in a concise manner.
- ✓ Example: Provide essential details without unnecessary information.

Use Professional Language:
- ✓ Do: Use formal and professional language in your emails.
- ✓ Example: "Dear [Customer's Name], I hope this email finds you well."

Proofread Before Sending:
- ✓ Do: Proofread your emails for grammar and spelling errors before hitting send.
- ✓ Example: "I appreciate your cooperation in resolving this issue."

Include Relevant Information:
- ✓ Do: Provide all necessary information for a comprehensive understanding.
- ✓ Example: Include account details and relevant context.

Use a Formal Closing:
- ✓ Do: Conclude your email with a formal closing and your name.
- ✓ Example: Best regards, [Your Full Name]

Include Contact Information:
- ✓ Do: Provide contact information for follow-up questions or concerns.
- ✓ Example: "Feel free to contact me at [Your Phone Number] for further assistance."

Follow Company Guidelines:
- ✓ Do: Adhere to company email policies and guidelines.
- ✓ Example: Respect any specific formatting or language requirements.

DON'Ts:

Use Unprofessional Email Addresses:
- ✓ Don't: Use personal or unprofessional email addresses.
- ✓ Example: johnnycool@emailprovider.com

Use Ambiguous Subject Lines:
- ✓ Don't: Use subject lines that are unclear or vague.
- ✓ Example: Subject: Help!

Skip Greetings:
- ✓ Don't: Skip greetings and start an email abruptly.
- ✓ Example: No greeting, straight to the issue.

Rambling or Excessive Detail:

- ✓ Don't: Include unnecessary details that may confuse the recipient.
- ✓ Example: Providing excessive back-story unrelated to the issue.

Use Informal Language:
- ✓ Don't: Use overly casual or informal language in professional emails.
- ✓ Example: *"Hey there, can you help me out?"*

Neglect Proofreading:
- ✓ Don't: Send emails without proofreading for errors.
- ✓ Example*: "I appreciate your cooperation in resolving this issue."*

Omitting Important Details:
- ✓ Don't: Forget to include crucial information needed for resolution.
- ✓ Example: Failing to provide an account number for reference.

Overuse of Jargon:
- ✓ Don't: Use excessive technical jargon that may confuse customers.
- ✓ Example: Using acronyms or terms without explanation.

Unprofessional Closing:
- ✓ Don't: Conclude emails abruptly without a proper closing.
- ✓ Example: Regards, [First Name]

Ignoring Company Policies:
- ✓ Don't: Disregard company email policies or guidelines.
- ✓ Example: Sending sensitive information without proper authorization.

By adhering to these DO's and avoiding the DON'Ts, help desk personnel can maintain a high level of professionalism in their email communication, ensuring clarity, effectiveness, and a positive customer experience.

Continuous Improvement and Teamwork

In the dynamic landscape of customer service, the commitment to continuous improvement and fostering a culture of teamwork is indispensable. This chapter explores the significance of the CARE Principle, emphasizing the importance of attitude and stress management. It also delves into the essential role of teamwork, discussing strategies for mobilizing employees and implementing tools for continuous improvement.

The CARE Principle

Importance of Attitude in Customer Service

Attitude is the linchpin of exceptional customer service. It transcends technical skills, shaping the customer's perception and overall experience. Consider a scenario where a customer interacts with a support representative facing technical difficulties. A positive attitude, expressed through empathy, active listening, and a genuine desire to assist, can transform a potentially frustrating situation into a positive experience.

Action Plan: Conduct attitude training sessions focusing on empathy, effective communication, and maintaining a positive mindset. Incorporate role-playing exercises to simulate real-world scenarios, allowing staff to practice and internalize positive attitudes.

What a HELP DESK Person can do to improve constantly on their Attitude

Improving and maintaining a positive attitude is crucial for help desk professionals in delivering exceptional customer service. Here are several actions they can take to continuously enhance their attitude:

1. Self-Reflection:
   - ✓ Action: Regularly reflect on personal attitudes and reactions.
   - ✓ Example: Ask, *"How did I handle that challenging situation, and how can I approach it differently next time?"*
2. Positive Affirmations:
   - ✓ Action: Start the day with positive affirmations.
   - ✓ Example: Repeat affirmations like *"I am capable, and I can handle any challenge with a positive mindset."*
3. Continuous Learning:
   - ✓ Action: Stay updated on industry trends and best practices.
   - ✓ Example: Attend workshops or online courses to enhance skills and knowledge, fostering confidence.
4. Gratitude Practice:
   - ✓ Action: Cultivate gratitude for positive aspects of work.
   - ✓ Example: Regularly acknowledge and appreciate successful resolutions and satisfied customers.
5. Effective Stress Management:
   - ✓ Action: Develop healthy stress management techniques.
   - ✓ Example: Practice deep breathing exercises or take short breaks during busy periods to reset.
6. Empathy Development:
   - ✓ Action: Work on understanding and empathizing with customers.

✓ Example: Put oneself in the customer's shoes to better comprehend their perspective.

7. Seek Constructive Feedback:
   ✓ Action: Request feedback from supervisors or colleagues.
   ✓ Example: Ask for specific examples of positive interactions and areas for improvement.

8. Regular Goal Setting:
   ✓ Action: Set achievable and realistic goals.
   ✓ Example: Aim to handle a certain number of cases effectively each day.

9. Positive Visualization:
   ✓ Action: Visualize successful interactions and positive outcomes.
   ✓ Example: Picture a satisfied customer after resolving a complex issue.

10. Mindfulness Practices:
   ✓ Action: Incorporate mindfulness techniques into daily routines.
   ✓ Example: Practice mindfulness meditation to stay present and focused.

11. Effective Time Management:
   ✓ Action: Prioritize tasks and manage time efficiently.
   ✓ Example: Use tools like calendars and to-do lists to organize workload effectively.

12. Celebrate Small Wins:
   ✓ Action: Acknowledge and celebrate achievements, no matter how small.
   ✓ Example: Celebrate successfully handling a challenging call or resolving a complicated issue.

13. Open Communication:
   ✓ Action: Communicate openly with colleagues about challenges.

✓ Example: Share experiences and seek advice on maintaining a positive attitude during tough situations.
14. Adaptability:
   ✓ Action: Embrace change and stay adaptable.
   ✓ Example: Accept that each day brings new challenges and opportunities for growth.
15. Professional Development:
   ✓ Action: Invest in ongoing professional development.
   ✓ Example: Attend conferences, webinars, or industry events to stay inspired and informed.
16. Team Collaboration:
   ✓ Action: Foster a positive team environment.
   ✓ Example: Collaborate with colleagues, share successes, and support each other during challenging times.
17. Customer-Centric Focus:
   ✓ Action: Keep the customer's needs at the forefront of interactions.
   ✓ Example: Remind oneself that each interaction is an opportunity to make a positive impact on a customer.
18. Set Boundaries:
   ✓ Action: Establish clear work-life boundaries.
   ✓ Example: Avoid bringing personal stressors into work and vice versa.

By consistently practicing these actions, help desk professionals can cultivate and sustain a positive attitude, contributing to improved job satisfaction, enhanced customer interactions, and overall professional growth.

Coping with Stress in the Service Industry

The service industry is inherently demanding, often requiring employees to navigate challenging situations. Coping with stress is a crucial skill. For example, in a busy restaurant, waitstaff may encounter high-pressure situations during peak hours. Implementing stress management techniques, such as mindfulness exercises or brief breaks, can help employees maintain composure and deliver exceptional service.

Action Plan: Develop a stress management program that includes mindfulness sessions, workshops on resilience, and techniques for maintaining composure in high-pressure situations. Encourage open communication about stressors and foster a supportive environment.

What a HELP DESK Person can do to cope up with Stress

Coping with stress is essential for help desk professionals who often deal with demanding situations. Here are strategies they can implement along with examples:

1. Mindfulness and Breathing Techniques:
   - ✓ Explanation: Practice mindfulness and deep breathing to stay present and manage stress.
   - ✓ Example: Take short breaks during the day to engage in deep breathing exercises, bringing attention back to the present moment.
2. Effective Time Management:
   - ✓ Explanation: Organize tasks and prioritize effectively to reduce overwhelm.

- ✓ Example: Use time management tools to create a schedule, breaking down larger tasks into smaller, more manageable steps.

3. Regular Physical Exercise:
   - ✓ Explanation: Engage in regular physical activity to release endorphins and reduce stress.
   - ✓ Example: Incorporate activities like walking, jogging, or yoga into the daily routine.

4. Establishing Work-Life Balance:
   - ✓ Explanation: Set clear boundaries between work and personal life.
   - ✓ Example: Avoid checking work emails outside of working hours to create a clear distinction between work and leisure time.

5. Positive Visualization:
   - ✓ Explanation: Visualize successful outcomes and positive scenarios.
   - ✓ Example: Imagine successfully resolving challenging customer issues and receiving positive feedback.

6. Seeking Support:
   - ✓ Explanation: Share feelings and concerns with trusted colleagues or friends.
   - ✓ Example: Discuss challenges with a peer to gain perspective and receive emotional support.

7. Mindful Eating:
   - ✓ Explanation: Pay attention to nutritional choices to support overall well-being.
   - ✓ Example: Choose balanced and nutritious meals, avoiding excessive caffeine or sugary snacks.

8. Setting Realistic Expectations:

- ✓ Explanation: Establish realistic goals and expectations for oneself.
- ✓ Example: Understand that perfection is unattainable, and focus on achieving realistic and achievable outcomes.

9. Regular Breaks:
- ✓ Explanation: Take short breaks during the workday to recharge.
- ✓ Example: Step away from the desk, stretch, or take a brief walk to refresh the mind and body.

10. Effective Communication:
- ✓ Explanation: Communicate openly with supervisors about workload and stressors.
- ✓ Example: Discuss workload concerns with a supervisor to explore possible solutions or adjustments.

11. Implementing Relaxation Techniques:
- ✓ Explanation: Incorporate relaxation techniques such as meditation or progressive muscle relaxation.
- ✓ Example: Dedicate a few minutes each day to practice relaxation exercises to reduce stress levels.

12. Humor and Positive Outlook:
- ✓ Explanation: Find humor in situations and maintain a positive outlook.
- ✓ Example: Use light-heartedness and humor to diffuse tense situations, creating a more positive atmosphere.

13. Continual Learning and Skill Development:
- ✓ Explanation: Invest time in learning new skills and staying updated in the field.
- ✓ Example: Attend training sessions or workshops to enhance skills, fostering a sense of accomplishment and growth.

14. Utilizing Employee Assistance Programs (EAP):
   ✓ Explanation: Explore available support services provided by the employer.
   ✓ Example: Access counseling services offered through EAP for professional assistance with stress management.
15. Regular Reflection and Goal Setting:
   ✓ Explanation: Reflect on accomplishments and set realistic goals.
   ✓ Example: Take time at the end of each week to review achievements and set achievable goals for the upcoming week.
16. Implementing a Relaxation Space:
   ✓ Explanation: Create a designated space for relaxation and stress relief.
   ✓ Example: Set up a comfortable corner with calming elements where employees can take short breaks.
17. Limiting Multitasking:
   ✓ Explanation: Focus on one task at a time to reduce stress associated with multitasking.
   ✓ Example: Prioritize tasks and dedicate focused attention to each before moving on to the next.
18. Embracing Change:
   ✓ Explanation: Cultivate an adaptive mindset and embrace change positively.
   ✓ Example: View challenges as opportunities for growth and learning rather than stressors.

By incorporating these coping strategies into their routine, help desk professionals can effectively manage stress, maintain overall well-being, and enhance their resilience in the face of demanding work situations.

Teamwork in Customer Service

Mobilizing Employees to Deliver Exceptional Service

Exceptional customer service is a collective effort that requires effective teamwork. Mobilizing employees to deliver outstanding service involves fostering a shared commitment to the customer's satisfaction. Imagine a scenario where an airline successfully manages a last-minute flight change for a passenger. This accomplishment is a result of seamless collaboration between various departments, from reservations to ground staff, highlighting the power of teamwork.

Action Plan: Implement cross-departmental training programs to enhance understanding and collaboration. Foster a culture where employees recognize and appreciate the contributions of their colleagues. Recognize and reward collaborative efforts to reinforce the importance of teamwork.

What can be done to Mobilize Employees to Deliver Exceptional Service

Mobilizing employees to deliver exceptional service involves empowering and motivating them to go above and beyond in meeting customer needs. Here are strategies with examples on how to achieve this:

1. Clear Vision and Mission:
   - ✓ Explanation: Communicate a compelling vision and mission that emphasizes the importance of exceptional service.
   - ✓ Example: Clearly articulate the company's commitment to providing unparalleled service and align it with broader organizational goals.

2. Leadership Support and Modeling:
   - ✓ Explanation: Leadership should exemplify the desired service standards to inspire employees.
   - ✓ Example: Executives actively engage with customers, showcasing the desired level of service in their interactions.
3. Empowerment and Autonomy:
   - ✓ Explanation: Grant employees the autonomy to make decisions and take initiative in serving customers.
   - ✓ Example: Customer service representatives have the authority to resolve issues up to a certain financial limit without seeking managerial approval.
4. Continuous Training and Development:
   - ✓ Explanation: Invest in ongoing training to equip employees with the necessary skills and knowledge.
   - ✓ Example: Regular workshops on effective communication and problem-solving to enhance customer service skills.
5. Recognition and Rewards:
   - ✓ Explanation: Acknowledge and reward employees for delivering exceptional service.
   - ✓ Example: Implement a monthly recognition program highlighting employees who received positive customer feedback.
6. Customer-Centric Culture:
   - ✓ Explanation: Foster a culture where everyone understands the value of exceptional customer service.
   - ✓ Example: Integrate customer-centric values into the organization's core values and highlight them in internal communications.

7. Open Communication Channels:
   - ✓ Explanation: Encourage open communication between employees and management.
   - ✓ Example: Regularly solicit feedback from frontline staff on customer challenges and incorporate their insights into service improvements.
8. Team Collaboration:
   - ✓ Explanation: Facilitate collaboration among team members to share best practices.
   - ✓ Example: Establish a platform for employees to share success stories and learnings from challenging customer interactions.
9. Customer Feedback Loop:
   - ✓ Explanation: Establish a system for employees to receive direct feedback from customers.
   - ✓ Example: Implement post-service surveys or feedback forms to collect insights on customer experiences.
10. Setting Service Standards:
   - ✓ Explanation: Define clear service standards and expectations for all employees.
   - ✓ Example: Develop a service charter outlining specific behaviors and actions expected from employees in customer interactions.
11. Investing in Technology:
   - ✓ Explanation: Provide employees with the tools and technology needed to deliver efficient service.
   - ✓ Example: Implement a customer relationship management (CRM) system to streamline customer interactions and information management.
12. Customer Journey Mapping:

- ✓ Explanation: Help employees understand the customer journey to anticipate needs.
- ✓ Example: Conduct workshops to map out typical customer interactions, identifying pain points and opportunities for improvement.

13. Performance Metrics and KPIs:
- ✓ Explanation: Establish key performance indicators (KPIs) aligned with exceptional service goals.
- ✓ Example: Track metrics such as customer satisfaction scores, resolution times, and positive feedback.

14. Customer Service Rituals:
- ✓ Explanation: Develop rituals that emphasize the importance of exceptional service.
- ✓ Example: Weekly team huddles where employees share positive customer stories and discuss ways to enhance service.

15. Celebrating Service Milestones:
- ✓ Explanation: Celebrate milestones related to exceptional service achievements.
- ✓ Example: Host a yearly event recognizing employees who consistently provide outstanding service over an extended period.

16. Cross-Functional Collaboration:
- ✓ Explanation: Encourage collaboration between different departments to ensure a unified approach to customer service.
- ✓ Example: Establish cross-functional teams to address customer pain points that may involve multiple departments.

17. Regular Service Training Refreshers:
- ✓ Explanation: Provide regular refresher courses to reinforce service principles.

✓ Example: Quarterly workshops focusing on specific aspects of customer service, such as empathy or effective problem-solving.

18. Flexibility and Adaptability:
    ✓ Explanation: Encourage flexibility and adaptability in responding to unique customer needs.
    ✓ Example: Allow employees to tailor solutions based on individual customer preferences within the established service guidelines.

By implementing these strategies, organizations can create a culture that mobilizes employees to consistently deliver exceptional service, resulting in increased customer satisfaction and loyalty.

Understanding Customer Behavior

In the intricate world of customer service, understanding and navigating customer behavior is a cornerstone for success. This chapter delves into behavioral analysis, emphasizing the importance of understanding oneself and others, identifying various customer types, and providing strategies for managing difficult people and sensitive situations.

Behavioral Analysis

Understanding Self and Others

At the heart of effective customer service lies the ability to understand oneself and others. Self-awareness allows customer service professionals to adapt their communication styles, empathize with customers, and build rapport. Likewise, understanding the diverse personalities and preferences of customers is crucial for tailoring interactions. Consider a scenario where a customer service representative, through self-awareness, recognizes their own communication tendencies and adjusts them to align with a customer's preferred style, creating a more harmonious interaction.

Action Plan: Implement personality assessments or communication style workshops for customer service staff. Encourage self-reflection to enhance self-awareness and provide training on recognizing and adapting to different customer communication styles.

A Personality Assessment for Customer Service Staff

Personality assessments for customer service staff can help identify individuals with traits that align with the demands of the role. Here's a template with examples of a personality assessment for customer service:

Personality Assessment for Customer Service Staff

Instructions: Please rate the following statements on a scale of 1 to 5, with 1 being strongly disagree and 5 being strongly agree. Be honest and respond based on your natural tendencies.

Communication Skills

I am comfortable communicating with individuals from diverse backgrounds.

1 (Strongly Disagree) | 2 | 3 | 4 | 5 (Strongly Agree)

I can convey information clearly and concisely.

1 | 2 | 3 | 4 | 5

I enjoy engaging in active listening during conversations.

1 | 2 | 3 | 4 | 5

Empathy and Understanding

I find it easy to understand and empathize with the concerns of others.

1 | 2 | 3 | 4 | 5

I am patient and can handle challenging situations with composure.

1 | 2 | 3 | 4 | 5

I genuinely enjoy helping others and solving their problems.

1 | 2 | 3 | 4 | 5

Adaptability and Flexibility

I can adapt quickly to changes in procedures or customer needs.

1 | 2 | 3 | 4 | 5

I remain calm and composed under pressure.

1 | 2 | 3 | 4 | 5

I am open to learning new skills to improve my performance.

1 | 2 | 3 | 4 | 5

Team Collaboration

I enjoy working collaboratively with colleagues to achieve common goals.

1 | 2 | 3 | 4 | 5

I am willing to share my knowledge and expertise with team members.

1 | 2 | 3 | 4 | 5

I can effectively communicate and coordinate with other departments.

1 | 2 | 3 | 4 | 5

Problem-Solving Skills

I am adept at identifying and resolving customer issues independently.

1 | 2 | 3 | 4 | 5

I enjoy finding creative solutions to unique customer challenges.

1 | 2 | 3 | 4 | 5

I can analyze situations quickly and make informed decisions.

1 | 2 | 3 | 4 | 5

Professionalism and Work Ethic

I consistently meet deadlines and complete tasks efficiently.

1 | 2 | 3 | 4 | 5

I maintain a positive attitude even in challenging work situations.

1 | 2 | 3 | 4 | 5
I take personal responsibility for my actions and outcomes.
1 | 2 | 3 | 4 | 5
Overall Fit for Customer Service Role
I believe my personality aligns well with the demands of a customer service role.
1 | 2 | 3 | 4 | 5
I am committed to continuous improvement in my customer service skills.
1 | 2 | 3 | 4 | 5

Scoring:
Sum the scores for each section to assess strengths and areas for improvement.
A higher total score indicates a strong alignment with the desired traits for customer service.

This template can be customized based on specific competencies or qualities important for the organization's customer service roles. Adjust statements or add new sections as needed.

Identifying Different Customer Types

Customers come in various shapes and sizes, each with unique needs, expectations, and communication styles. Identifying different customer types is essential for tailoring interactions. For example, a tech support agent dealing with a novice user might need to adopt a more patient and instructional approach, while a seasoned user might prefer a more technical and concise explanation.

Action Plan: Develop customer personas representing typical users. Train customer service staff to recognize these personas and adjust their communication and service delivery accordingly. Encourage staff to share insights about recurring customer types for continuous improvement.

A Template for the Customer Personas Representing Typical Users

Creating customer personas helps in understanding and empathizing with different user segments. Below is a template with examples for customer personas representing typical users:

Customer Persona Template
- ✓ Persona Name: [Give the persona a representative name]
- ✓ Demographics:

Age: [e.g., 28]
Gender: [e.g., Female]
Location: [e.g., Urban, Suburban, Rural]
Occupation: [e.g., Marketing Professional]
Background:

Education: [e.g., Bachelor's in Business Administration]
Family Status: [e.g., Single, Married, Parent]
Income Level: [e.g., Middle-income]
Personal Attributes:
Hobbies/Interests: [e.g., Reading, Fitness, Travel]
Preferred Communication Channels: [e.g., Social Media, Email, Phone]
Professional Attributes:
Industry: [e.g., Technology]
Job Role: [e.g., Software Developer]
Level of Expertise: [e.g., Entry-Level, Mid-Level]
Goals and Motivations:
Personal Goals: [e.g., Achieving Work-Life Balance]
Professional Goals: [e.g., Learning New Programming Languages]
Challenges: [e.g., Limited Time for Personal Hobbies]
Pain Points:
Challenges with Current Solutions: [e.g., Finding Reliable Fitness Apps]
Frustrations: [e.g., Lack of Time Management]
User Behavior:
Preferred Shopping Habits: [e.g., Online Shopping, In-Store Purchases]
Tech-Savvy Level: [e.g., Early Adopter, Moderate]
Customer Journey:
Awareness Stage:
How does the persona typically become aware of a product or service?
[e.g., Through online reviews, social media recommendations]
Consideration Stage:
What factors influence their decision-making process?

[e.g., Reviews from trusted sources, product features]
Decision Stage:
How does the persona make the final decision to purchase or engage?
[e.g., Discounts or promotions, free trials]
Preferred Features and Benefits:
Key Features Sought: [e.g., User-friendly interface, Time-saving features]
Primary Benefits Desired: [e.g., Increased productivity, Improved well-being]
How Our Product/Service Helps:
Unique Selling Proposition (USP):
[e.g., Our fitness app offers personalized workout plans that fit into busy schedules, helping users achieve their fitness goals efficiently.]

Example Customer Persona: Sarah, the Software Developer
Demographics:
- ✓ Age: 32
- ✓ Gender: Female
- ✓ Location: Urban
- ✓ Occupation: Software Developer

Background:
- ✓ Education: Master's in Computer Science
- ✓ Family Status: Single
- ✓ Income Level: Middle-income

Personal Attributes:
- ✓ Hobbies/Interests: Reading, Yoga, Travel
- ✓ Preferred Communication Channels: Email, Social Media

Professional Attributes:
- ✓ Industry: Technology
- ✓ Job Role: Software Developer

✓ Level of Expertise: Mid-Level

Goals and Motivations:
- ✓ Personal Goals: Achieving Work-Life Balance
- ✓ Professional Goals: Learning New Programming Languages
- ✓ Challenges: Limited Time for Personal Hobbies

Pain Points:
- ✓ Challenges with Current Solutions: Finding Reliable Fitness Apps
- ✓ Frustrations: Lack of Time Management

User Behavior:
- ✓ Preferred Shopping Habits: Online Shopping
- ✓ Tech-Savvy Level: Moderate

Customer Journey:

Awareness Stage: Through online reviews and recommendations from colleagues.

Consideration Stage: Influenced by positive reviews and features that align with her fitness goals.

Decision Stage: Chooses based on promotional discounts and a user-friendly interface.

Preferred Features and Benefits:
- ✓ Key Features Sought: User-friendly interface, Time-saving features
- ✓ Primary Benefits Desired: Increased productivity, Improved well-being

How Our Product/Service Helps:
- ✓ Unique Selling Proposition (USP): Our fitness app offers personalized workout plans that fit into busy schedules, helping users like Sarah achieve their fitness goals efficiently.

This template can be adapted and expanded based on the specific needs and characteristics of different customer segments. Creating multiple personas allows businesses to tailor their products or services to better meet the diverse needs of their user base.

Managing Difficult People and Sensitive Situations

Techniques for Dealing Assertively

Difficult people and sensitive situations are inevitable in customer service. Dealing assertively is a crucial skill in maintaining professionalism and resolving conflicts. Picture a scenario where a customer expresses dissatisfaction with a product. An assertive response involves actively listening to the customer's concerns, acknowledging their feelings, and proposing constructive solutions.

Action Plan: Provide assertiveness training for customer service staff, emphasizing active listening, empathy, and conflict resolution techniques. Role-play various challenging scenarios to allow staff to practice and refine their assertiveness skills.

Resolving Conflicts Professionally

Conflict resolution is an art that requires finesse and professionalism. Resolving conflicts professionally involves de-escalating tense situations, finding common ground, and proposing mutually beneficial solutions. Consider a customer service representative handling a billing dispute. A professional conflict resolution approach involves calmly addressing the issue, providing explanations or alternatives, and ensuring the customer feels heard and respected.

Action Plan: Develop a conflict resolution framework that aligns with the company's values. Provide training on de-escalation techniques, effective communication during conflicts, and strategies for finding common ground. Establish a feedback mechanism to continuously refine conflict resolution processes.

A Template for Conflict Resolution Framework Aligns with Company's Values.

A conflict resolution framework is crucial for maintaining a positive work environment. Below is an example and template for a conflict resolution framework aligned with company values:

Conflict Resolution Framework

Company Values:

[List the core values of the company, e.g., Transparency, Collaboration, Respect, Integrity]

Step 1: Acknowledge the Conflict

- ✓ Objective: Recognize and accept that a conflict exists.
- ✓ Example: *"At [Company Name], we value transparency. If you find yourself in a situation where there is a conflict, it's important to acknowledge it openly and honestly. Recognizing the conflict is the first step in addressing and resolving it."*

Step 2: Understand Perspectives

- ✓ Objective: Encourage individuals involved to express their viewpoints.
- ✓ Example: *"Our commitment to collaboration means that everyone's perspective is valued. Take the time to understand each party's point of view. This may involve open discussions, active listening, and empathy to grasp the underlying concerns."*

Step 3: Identify Common Ground

- ✓ Objective: Find areas of agreement and shared interests.

✓ Example: *"Respect is one of our fundamental values. Look for common ground where conflicting parties can agree. Identify shared goals or interests that can serve as a foundation for resolution."*

Step 4: Collaborative Problem-Solving
✓ Objective: Encourage parties to work together on finding solutions.
✓ Example: *"Integrity is key in our interactions. Encourage collaborative problem-solving. Invite the conflicting parties to brainstorm solutions together. This ensures that everyone is actively involved in finding resolutions that align with our values."*

Step 5: Seek Mediation if Necessary
✓ Objective: Involve a neutral third party to facilitate resolution.
✓ Example: *"If conflicts persist, we emphasize the importance of seeking mediation. This neutral third party can guide the resolution process, ensuring fairness and adherence to our values of respect and integrity."*

Step 6: Implement and Review Solutions
✓ Objective: Put agreed-upon solutions into action and assess their effectiveness.
✓ Example: *"Transparency and accountability are vital to our success. Once a resolution is agreed upon, implement the solutions promptly. Periodically review the effectiveness of the implemented solutions to ensure a lasting resolution."*

Step 7: Learn and Improve
✓ Objective: Emphasize continuous improvement based on conflict experiences.

    ✓ Example: *"We value a culture of learning and improvement. After conflict resolution, take the opportunity to reflect. What lessons can be learned from this conflict, and how can our processes be enhanced to prevent similar issues in the future?"*

Conflict Resolution Framework Template
Step 1: Acknowledge the Conflict
    ✓ Objective: [Insert Objective]
    ✓ Example: [Insert Example]
Step 2: Understand Perspectives
    ✓ Objective: [Insert Objective]
    ✓ Example: [Insert Example]
Step 3: Identify Common Ground
    ✓ Objective: [Insert Objective]
    ✓ Example: [Insert Example]
Step 4: Collaborative Problem-Solving
    ✓ Objective: [Insert Objective]
    ✓ Example: [Insert Example]
Step 5: Seek Mediation if Necessary
    ✓ Objective: [Insert Objective]
    ✓ Example: [Insert Example]
Step 6: Implement and Review Solutions
    ✓ Objective: [Insert Objective]
    ✓ Example: [Insert Example]
Step 7: Learn and Improve
    ✓ Objective: [Insert Objective]
    ✓ Example: [Insert Example]

This template can be customized to match the specific values and goals of your company. It provides a structured approach to conflict resolution that aligns with the organization's principles, fostering a positive and collaborative workplace culture.

Understanding Users and Categorizing Them

Understanding users and categorizing them based on their needs is crucial for tailoring services and support effectively. Here are steps to understand users, identify user categories, and determine appropriate services for each category:

1. Conduct User Surveys and Interviews:

Steps:

- ✓ Create surveys to gather feedback on user experiences.
- ✓ Conduct interviews to understand specific challenges and preferences.
- ✓ Analyze responses to identify common themes and concerns.

Example:

- ✓ Survey users on their satisfaction with current IT services.
- ✓ Interview department heads to identify unique needs within their teams.

2. Analyze User Behavior and Patterns:

Steps:

- ✓ Utilize analytics tools to track user interactions with systems.
- ✓ Identify common pathways, preferences, and frequent support requests.
- ✓ Analyze user data to discern trends and usage patterns.

Example:

- ✓ Track which features of a software application are most frequently accessed.
- ✓ Identify peak usage times and potential system bottlenecks.

3. Create User Personas:

Steps:

- ✓ Develop fictional characters representing different user types.
- ✓ Assign characteristics, preferences, and challenges to each persona.
- ✓ Use personas to visualize and understand diverse user needs.

Example:

- ✓ Create personas like "Power User," "Occasional User," and "New Employee."
- ✓ Outline their specific requirements, technical proficiency, and pain points.

4. Segment Users Based on Roles and Responsibilities:

Steps:

- ✓ Identify distinct user roles within the organization.
- ✓ Understand the responsibilities and tasks associated with each role.
- ✓ Tailor services based on the unique needs of each role.

Example:

- ✓ Categorize users as "Administrative Staff," "Sales Team," and "Technical Support."
- ✓ Customize training programs for each role to enhance job-specific skills.

5. Evaluate User Skill Levels:

Steps:

- ✓ Assess the technical proficiency of users.
- ✓ Identify skill gaps and areas where additional training is required.
- ✓ Tailor support services to accommodate varying skill levels.

Example:

- ✓ Conduct IT proficiency assessments for employees.
- ✓ Offer targeted training sessions for users with specific skill deficiencies.

6. Assess Specific Departmental Needs:

Steps:
- ✓ Collaborate with department heads to understand department-specific requirements.
- ✓ Identify tools, applications, or workflows critical to each department.
- ✓ Align IT services to meet the unique needs of different departments.

Example:
- ✓ Work with the HR department to understand their software requirements.
- ✓ Provide specialized applications or configurations for the Finance team.

7. Implement User Feedback Mechanisms:

Steps:
- ✓ Establish channels for users to provide continuous feedback.
- ✓ Regularly review and analyze feedback for insights.
- ✓ Use feedback to refine services and address specific user concerns.

Example:
- ✓ Set up a dedicated email address for user feedback.
- ✓ Conduct periodic surveys to gather input on the effectiveness of support services.

8. Collaborate with User Representatives:

Steps:
- ✓ Appoint user representatives from different departments or user categories.

- ✓ Organize regular meetings to discuss challenges and improvement suggestions.
- ✓ Leverage user representatives as liaisons between IT and end-users.

Example:

- ✓ Form a user advisory group with representatives from various teams.
- ✓ Discuss upcoming system changes or new software implementations.

9. Prioritize User Needs and Expectations:

Steps:

- ✓ Prioritize user needs based on their impact on productivity and satisfaction.
- ✓ Allocate resources to address high-priority user requirements.
- ✓ Communicate the prioritization process to manage user expectations.

Example:

- ✓ Identify critical applications and ensure they receive priority support.
- ✓ Communicate clearly about the timeline for addressing less urgent requests.

10. Create Tailored Support Packages:

Steps:

- ✓ Develop support packages aligned with user categories.
- ✓ Clearly define the scope of support for each package.
- ✓ Communicate available services and support levels to users.

Example:

- ✓ Offer a premium support package for power users requiring rapid response times.
- ✓ Provide self-service options for users with routine and non-urgent inquiries.

Understanding users, categorizing them appropriately, and tailoring services to meet their unique needs enhance overall satisfaction, efficiency, and collaboration within the organization. Regularly revisit these steps to adapt to evolving user requirements and technological advancements.

Typical Incident Management Process

The Incident Management Process is crucial for promptly and effectively resolving issues that arise within an organization. Below are the step-by-step actions involved in a typical incident process, including tracking incidents, taking ownership, and follow-up, with examples:

1. Incident Identification:

Action:

Users or automated monitoring systems identify and report incidents.

Example:

An employee reports that they are unable to access a critical software application.

2. Incident Logging:

Action:

Help desk professionals log the incident details in a centralized system.

Example:

Logging the incident includes capturing information such as user details, a brief description of the issue, and any relevant error messages.

3. Incident Categorization:

Action:

Classify the incident into predefined categories for efficient handling.

Example:

Categorize the incident as a "Login Issue" or a "Software Functionality Problem."

4. Incident Prioritization:

Action:

Assess the impact and urgency of the incident to determine its priority.

Example:

Prioritize a system outage affecting multiple users over an isolated issue for a single user.

5. Initial Diagnosis:

Action:

Conduct a preliminary investigation to identify the root cause.

Example:

Check system logs, user permissions, or recent changes that may be related to the reported issue.

6. Incident Ownership:

Action:

Assign ownership to a specific support agent or team.

Example:

Assign the incident to a level 1 support agent who specializes in basic troubleshooting.

7. Incident Escalation (if needed):

Action:

Escalate the incident to a higher support level if initial diagnosis is inconclusive.

Example:

Escalate a complex technical issue to level 2 support or the system administrator for in-depth analysis.

8. Resolution or Workaround:

Action:

Implement a solution or workaround to address the incident.

Example:

Provide the user with step-by-step instructions to reset their password, resolving the login issue temporarily.

9. Incident Closure:

Action:
Confirm with the user that the issue is resolved and close the incident.
Example:
Receive confirmation from the user that they can now access the software without any problems.
10. Incident Documentation:
Action:
Document the incident details, resolution steps, and any relevant findings.
Example:
Update the knowledge base with information on how the login issue was resolved for future reference.
11. User Communication:
Action:
Communicate the resolution to the user, providing any necessary follow-up instructions.
Example:
Send an email to the user confirming the resolution and advising on preventive measures.
12. Incident Review and Analysis:
Action:
Conduct a post-incident review to identify opportunities for improvement.
Example:
Analyze whether the incident could have been prevented and implement measures to enhance proactive support.
13. Follow-up (if needed):
Action:
Follow up with the user to ensure the incident resolution is satisfactory.
Example:

A support agent calls the user a few days later to confirm that they are still able to use the software without any issues.

14. Incident Tracking and Reporting:
Action:
Maintain a record of incidents for tracking and reporting purposes.
Example:
Generate monthly reports on the number of incidents, average resolution times, and recurring issues.

By following these steps, organizations can ensure a systematic and efficient incident management process, minimizing disruptions and providing timely support to users.

Implementing a Successful Help Desk Skills Initiative: Action Plan

Implementing a successful Help Desk Skills Initiative requires careful planning and execution. Below is a detailed action plan with steps, actions, and examples to guide organizations in this initiative:

Action Plan: Implementing a Successful Help Desk Skills Initiative

Step 1: Assess Current Skills and Needs

Actions:

- ✓ Skills Assessment: Conduct a thorough assessment of the current skills of help desk personnel.
- ✓ Example: Use surveys, interviews, and performance evaluations to understand existing skill levels.
- ✓ Identify Gaps: Identify skill gaps and areas that require improvement.
- ✓ Example: Analyze customer feedback, ticket resolution times, and common challenges faced by help desk staff.

Step 2: Define Clear Objectives and Outcomes

Actions:

- ✓ Set Clear Goals: Define specific, measurable, achievable, relevant, and time-bound (SMART) goals for the initiative.
- ✓ Example: Increase customer satisfaction ratings by 15% within the next six months.
- ✓ Outline Desired Outcomes: Clearly outline the expected outcomes and benefits of improved help desk skills.

✓ Example: Faster resolution times, reduced escalations, and increased customer loyalty.

Step 3: Develop a Customized Training Program
Actions:
- ✓ Identify Training Topics: Based on the assessment, identify key training topics such as communication skills, problem-solving, and technical knowledge.
- ✓ Example: Create modules on effective telephone communication, handling difficult customers, and technical troubleshooting.
- ✓ Select Training Methods: Choose suitable training methods, including workshops, online courses, and role-playing exercises.
- ✓ Example: Conduct interactive workshops for hands-on learning and utilize online modules for self-paced training.

Step 4: Align Training with Company Values
Actions:
- ✓ Integrate Core Values: Ensure that training content aligns with the organization's core values.
- ✓ Example: Emphasize values like customer-centricity, transparency, and continuous improvement in training materials.
- ✓ Use Real-World Scenarios: Develop training scenarios that reflect real-world help desk situations.
- ✓ Example: Simulate customer interactions with common issues to provide practical learning experiences.

Step 5: Implement Training with a Practical Approach
Actions:

✓ Schedule Regular Training Sessions: Establish a training schedule that allows employees to participate without disrupting daily operations.
✓ Example: Conduct weekly training sessions during non-peak hours.
✓ Include Practical Exercises: Incorporate practical exercises and simulations to reinforce learning.
✓ Example: Have trainees role-play challenging customer interactions to apply new skills.

Step 6: Empower Frontline Staff

Actions:

✓ Encourage Proactive Problem-Solving: Foster a culture that empowers help desk staff to proactively address issues.
✓ Example: Recognize and reward employees who successfully resolve customer problems independently.
✓ Provide Decision-Making Authority: Grant frontline staff decision-making authority within defined limits.
✓ Example: Allow them to offer compensation or escalate issues based on established guidelines.

Step 7: Monitor and Measure Progress

Actions:

✓ Establish Key Performance Indicators (KPIs): Define KPIs to measure the success of the initiative.
✓ Example: Monitor ticket resolution times, customer satisfaction scores, and the number of escalations.

✓ Implement Regular Assessments: Conduct periodic assessments to track progress and identify areas for improvement.

✓ Example: Use monthly assessments to gauge skill development and address any emerging challenges.

Step 8: Provide Ongoing Support and Resources

Actions:

✓ Create a Knowledge Base: Develop a comprehensive knowledge base to support ongoing learning.

✓ Example: Document common issues, troubleshooting steps, and best practices for quick reference.

✓ Offer Continuing Education Opportunities: Provide opportunities for continuous learning, such as advanced training modules and certifications.

✓ Example: Sponsor employees to obtain relevant certifications in customer service and technical skills.

Step 9: Solicit Feedback and Adapt

Actions:

✓ Gather Employee Feedback: Regularly seek feedback from help desk staff on the effectiveness of the training program.

✓ Example: Conduct surveys or hold feedback sessions to understand their experiences and suggestions.

✓ Adapt the Program: Use feedback to make necessary adjustments and improvements to the training initiative.

✓ Example: Modify training content based on emerging challenges or changing customer needs.

Step 10: Recognize and Celebrate Success
Actions:
- ✓ Acknowledge Achievements: Recognize and celebrate achievements and improvements in help desk skills.
- ✓ Example: Publicly acknowledge individuals or teams that demonstrate exceptional customer service.
- ✓ Share Success Stories: Share success stories with the entire organization to highlight the positive impact of improved help desk skills.
- ✓ Example: Feature success stories in internal communications or company meetings.

Step 11: Conduct Regular Reviews and Updates
Actions:
- ✓ Regularly Review Training Materials: Periodically review and update training materials to keep them current and relevant.
- ✓ Example: Incorporate new technologies or industry best practices into the training curriculum.
- ✓ Adapt to Changing Needs: Stay flexible and adapt the initiative to address evolving customer expectations and industry trends.
- ✓ Example: Introduce new modules to address emerging challenges or trends in customer service.

By following this comprehensive action plan, organizations can successfully implement a Help Desk Skills Initiative that enhances the capabilities of their customer support teams, resulting in improved customer satisfaction and loyalty.

Empowering Help Desk Professionals for Excellence in Customer Service

The journey through this comprehensive program has been a transformative experience for participants, equipping them with the multifaceted skills needed to excel in the complex and dynamic realm of customer service. As we conclude this program, it is evident that participants are now empowered to fulfill the critical responsibilities of the help desk with confidence and proficiency.

The core objectives of the program were not only met but surpassed, with participants gaining a deep understanding of the pivotal role they play in shaping a positive customer experience. The program focused on instilling a positive attitude, enhancing personal qualities, fostering effective communication, and equipping participants with the ability to navigate challenging situations with finesse.

Positive Attitude and Personal Qualities:

One of the central pillars of the program was the cultivation of a positive attitude. Participants engaged in discussions and practical workshops that highlighted the transformative impact of a positive mindset on customer interactions. Through various activities, they learned to embody professionalism, empathy, and resilience, creating a welcoming and supportive environment for customers.

The emphasis on personal qualities extended beyond mere professionalism. Through role-plays and real-life scenarios, participants honed their interpersonal skills, recognizing the importance of warmth, sincerity, and genuine care in customer interactions. Creating and presenting a professional image, as well as personal grooming, were explored as integral components of projecting a positive and trustworthy image to customers.

Effective Communication and Handling Difficult Situations:

The program delved deep into the nuances of communication, recognizing it as a cornerstone of exceptional customer service. Through role-plays and action learning, participants refined their communication skills, ensuring clarity, empathy, and active listening in every interaction. The training encompassed telephone techniques, face-to-face interactions, and internet communication, providing participants with a comprehensive toolkit for seamless communication across diverse platforms.

Moreover, participants gained valuable insights and strategies for handling difficult situations. Techniques for dealing assertively and resolving conflicts professionally were explored in depth. By engaging in practical workshops, participants became adept at turning complaints into opportunities for improvement and empowering frontline staff to address issues proactively.

Proficiency in Telephone and Internet Skills:

The program recognized the evolving landscape of customer interactions, placing significant emphasis on mastering telephone and internet skills. Through simulated scenarios and hands-on exercises, participants developed the proficiency to navigate the nuances of telephone conversations and email interactions. They honed the art of timely and effective responses in the digital realm, understanding the importance of written communication etiquette.

Holistic Skill Development through Varied Training Methods:

The success of this program lies in its holistic approach to skill development. By employing diverse training methods, including discussions, action learning, role-plays, and practical workshops, participants engaged in immersive learning experiences. The integration of these methods ensured that theoretical knowledge was complemented by hands-on application, reinforcing the learning objectives.

Result: Increased Confidence, Enthusiasm, and Commitment:

The program's impact extends beyond the acquisition of skills; it is reflected in the increased confidence, enthusiasm, and commitment of the participants. Armed with a newfound skill set, they are poised to contribute significantly to the company's positive image and overall success. The commitment to delivering exceptional service has become ingrained in their professional ethos.

In essence, this program has not only equipped help desk professionals with the necessary tools for success but has also fostered a culture of continuous improvement. The ripple effect of empowered and skilled individuals will undoubtedly resonate throughout the organization, creating a positive feedback loop of excellence in customer service.

As we conclude this program, it is our belief that the participants, now armed with a comprehensive skill set, are not just customer service professionals; they are ambassadors of exceptional service, ready to elevate the customer experience and contribute to the ongoing success of their organization.

Conclusion:
Elevating Your Helpdesk Journey

As we reach the conclusion of this comprehensive guide on Professional Helpdesk Skills, take a moment to reflect on the transformative journey we've embarked upon together. From the significance of first impressions to the intricacies of telephone techniques, personal interactions, and internet communication, we've delved into the multifaceted world of customer service.

A Recap of Key Insights

Throughout these pages, we've uncovered the statistics that underscore the value of exceptional customer service. The stories of businesses losing customers due to dissatisfaction and the financial impact of neglecting customer loyalty serve as poignant reminders of the stakes at play. As help desk professionals, your role is not just about resolving issues; it's about crafting experiences that leave lasting impressions.

Remember the Diamond Rule of Service – treat others as you want to be treated. This principle, rooted in empathy and respect, is the cornerstone of exceptional customer interactions. The C.A.R.E. Principle has guided us through understanding the current complaints culture, embracing complaints as opportunities for improvement, and empowering frontline staff to resolve issues with confidence.

Beyond Technicalities: The Human Element

As we navigated through the intricacies of telephone techniques, personal interactions, and internet communication, it became evident that customer service is not just a transactional exchange of information. It's a human connection forged through effective communication, genuine care, and a commitment to continuous improvement.

Your attitude matters. The way you cope with stress, handle difficult situations, and embrace a mindset of continuous improvement sets the tone for not just your success but the success of your entire team and organization.

Applying What You've Learned

Now, armed with a toolkit of skills, strategies, and insights, it's time to apply what you've learned. The action plans, examples, and practical exercises provided in each chapter are not merely theoretical constructs; they are invitations to step into the role of a customer service champion.

Encourage proactive problem-solving, empower your frontline staff, and remember that every interaction is an opportunity to exceed expectations. Use the knowledge gained here to not only address customer issues but to build relationships that endure.

A Commitment to Excellence

In the fast-paced world of customer service, excellence is not a destination; it's a commitment. Commit to continuous learning, embrace the challenges as opportunities for growth, and foster a culture of customer-centricity within your team and organization.

Your journey towards becoming a customer service maestro doesn't end here; it's an ongoing process of refinement and evolution. The skills you've honed are not just tools in your professional arsenal; they are catalysts for success, differentiating you in a competitive landscape.

Thank You for Joining Us
On behalf of the entire team behind this guide, I extend our sincere gratitude for joining us on this journey. May the skills you've cultivated here be the catalyst for your personal and professional growth. May your interactions be infused with empathy, your solutions be proactive, and your commitment to excellence be unwavering.

Here's to elevating your helpdesk journey and creating customer service experiences that leave an indelible mark.

About the Author
'GERARD ASSEY'

Gerard Assey is a Graduate in Economics, a PGD in Management (HRD) and holds a Doctorate in Leadership. Gerard holds several International Qualifications in Sales, Debt Collection, Training & Teaching, and is a 'Fellow' of the prestigious 'Institute of Sales & Marketing Management'-UK, a Certified NLP Practitioner, a 'Certified Trainer', an 'Accredited Management Teacher-Behavioral Sciences', a 'Certified Competency Facilitator', a 'Certified Management Consultant'- (the International credentials of a professional management consultant, awarded in accordance with global standards of the ICMCI); and a Certification from the University of Michigan in 'Successful Negotiation: Essential Strategies and Skills'

He is also a Member of the 'National Association of Sales Professionals' backed with several years experience in varied industries, both in India and Overseas. He also holds an 'Etiquette Consultant' Certification from the USA (by Sue Fox, Author of Best Seller: 'Business Etiquette for Dummies'. She has trained some of the top celebrities' world over). He was also a recipient of a scholarship for extensive training in Japan on 'Corporate Management for India'.

Gerard Assey is 'Founder & Chief Corporate Trainer' of the Group: **'Citius, Altius, Fortius Unlimited'**- an organization that **celebrated 20 years of Glorious Service** in 2021, focusing on 3 Core Competencies:

People. Performance. Profit; in functional areas of Sales & Marketing, HR & Organizational Development, covering Recruitment, Training & Consultancy!

Having managed organizations with large Sales Forces in India & Overseas, his specialization cover extensive areas of Sales Training (All levels - Presentation, Negotiation, Key/ Strategic Accounts Management & Managerial Skills for all sectors), Bid Proposal/ Capture Planning/ Management Trainings, Retail Sales, Customer Service & Customer Retention Programs, Training for Prevention & Collection of Debt, Self & Personal Development Programs (Time Management, Teamwork & Team Building, Business Etiquette & Personal Grooming, Leadership & Managerial Skills, People Management Skills, Train-the-Trainer etc), including preparation of Custom-designed Business Manuals for Internal (HR, Induction, and Sales etc) & External use (Instruction, User Manuals).

Gerard has successfully conducted over 6080 Trainings & Workshops (as of Feb '24) all across India, Middle East, Africa, Europe & S.E. Asia. Besides public programs conducted regularly, both in India & Overseas, he has some of the top names as clients whom he services from Single Owners to large Public & Government undertakings, covering all sectors, for their in-house needs.

His website: www.CollectionSkills.com is the only one in this part of the world to be featured in the 'Collections & Credit Risk Magazine-USA' under 'Who's Who in Training' and ranks TOP, along with other websites listed below on most search engines.

Gerard is author of 115 books already (Mar 2024)

A few of our business related books:

1. Bite-sized Bits on Commonsense Management
2. Heart to Heart on Life's Principles'
3. How to become a Successful Manager
4. The Sales Professionals' Master Workbook of S.Y.S.T.E.M.S
5. The Professional Business Email Etiquette Handbook & Guide
6. The Professional Business Video-Conferencing Etiquette Handbook & Guide
7. Professional Presentation Skills
8. Exceptional Customer Service
9. Professional Tele-Marketing Skills
10. Professional Debt Collection Skills
11. The G.R.E.A.T. Sales & Service Workbook
12. Sales Training Advantage for Results (*The Ultimate Sales Training Manual to enable you stand out as a S.T.A.R.*)
13. CEO Daily Planner & Organizer
14. The Sales Professionals' Master Daily Planner
15. The Professional Debt Collector's Master Daily Planner
16. My Daily Planner & Organizer
17. MY EMERGENCY INFORMATION RECORD (Family Emergency & Peace of Mind Planner)
18. The Ultimate Therapist & Counselors Planner and Organizer
19. Building an Ethical Workplace
20. Managing Relationships at Work
21. Managing Business Meetings Effectively
22. Effective Delegation Skills
23. Goal Setting for Success
24. B2B Selling by Email
25. Professional Business Etiquette & Grooming
26. Dining Etiquette & Table Manners
27. Effective Networking Skills
28. Grooming, Etiquette & Manners for Teens, Young Adults & Future Leaders
29. Inter-Personal Skills
30. Get Ready, Get Hired!
31. Selling in a Recession
32. Effective Receivables Management in an Economic Downturn!
33. Real Estate & Property Sales Training

34. Credit Sales & Accounts Receivable Management
35. Selling Skills for Real Estate & Property Advisors
36. Take G.R.E.A.T. C.A.R.E!
37. Spa, Salon & Health Club Selling Skills
38. Selling Travel, Holiday & MICE Services
39. Selling Skills for Spa's, Salons & Health Clubs
40. Retailing in Salons & Spas
41. Selling Holiday, Vacation, Tours & Packages
42. The Power of Sales Referrals
43. Selling Luxury
44. Technical Selling Skills
45. Financial Advisors Sales Training
46. Dealing with Burnout at Work Monopolize Your Markets
47. Selling to Affluent Customers
48. Growing up with Grace
49. Financial Selling Skills
50. *The Effective Manager's Guide: Key Skills to Thrive*
51. From Aspiring to Inspiring: A Guide for New Managers on the Rise
52. The Power of Focus
53. Selling with Integrity: Sell Like Jesus The Perfect Role Model!
54. 31 Habits of Champions: Your 31-Day Journey to Greatness
55. Rejecting Grasshopper Talk: From Grasshopper to Giant-Killer-*Defeating Giants Daily!*
56. Navigate the AI-Powered Future of Bid & Proposals: Up-Skill to Stay Relevant with Alternative Career Paths & Opportunities
57. Hiring Sales Winners
58. Present with Impact
59. Success Unlocked: *Breaking Free from Habits that Hold You Back*
60. Complaints to Cheers, Feedback to Gold: Mastering Complaints Management
61. Thriving Together: *Cultivating Diversity, Equity, and Inclusion*
62. Coaching Skills for Sales Managers
63. Soaring to Success in Business & Leadership: Swifter, Higher, Stronger!
64. From Classroom to Podium: A Student's Guide to Powerful Public Speaking & Presentation Skills

65. Developing Self-Discipline
66. The CEO's 31-Day Power Plan: Unlocking Success through Essential Traits
67. Credibility Matters
68. A Winning Attitude
69. Bid & Proposal Management Using AI
70. Sales Forecasting: A Practical & Proven Guide to Strategic Sales Forecasting
71. Elevate & Energize: *50 Dynamic & Fun Activities for Peak Workplace Morale*
72. 'Sales SOS! Sales on Fire! *30 Days to Conquer Chaos & the Nightmares of Success!*'
73. Mastering Sales Managerial Skills: *Building High-Performing Teams & Driving Exceptional Results*
74. Eagle-Eyed Leadership: Unleashing the Power of 31 Lessons from Eagles
75. The Ultimate Employee Training Guide: *Training Today, Leading Tomorrow*
76. Being More Accountable at Work
77. Creating a Culture of Continuous Improvement
78. Effective Questioning & Listening Skills
79. The Power of Value Selling
80. The Growth Mindset
81. Mastering Professional Help Desk Skills

Besides regularly contributing to business & trade journals, including international ones such as the 'Creative Training Techniques' and the 'Sales News' of the U.S.A, He is also a member of several prestigious bodies & trade associations, having participated in many Conferences & Workshops in India & Overseas.

Prior to his last assignment of leading & managing a large MNC as head, Gerard had a 3-year stint in the Middle East as a Consultant with a leading British Consultancy Firm.

As the past 'Official Country Representative' for the International Business Award- 'THE STEVIES'-(the business world's own Oscar) for about 4 years- he ensured a few Indian companies that qualify for the same every year!

Gerard can be contacted at:
Email: training@Sales-Training.in,training@CollectionSkills.com
Websites:

     www.Sales-Training.in
     www.EtiquetteWorks.in
     www.CollectionSkills.com
     www.RetailSalesTraining.in
     www.SalesTrainingIndia.com
     www.ManualPreparation.com
     www.TrainingWithPuppets.com
     www.FirstContactAcademy.com
     www.SalesAndMarketingRecruiter.com

Our TRAININGS that can help your team

- ✓ **Sales Effectiveness**: Selling Skills for any Sector: Service/ Logistics/ FMCG Realty/ Insurance & Finance/ Media/ SPA's, Health Clubs & Salons/ Key Account Management, Effective Negotiation Skills/ Bid & Proposal Management Skills/ Retail Sales Training: Any Sector (Auto, Jewelry, Clothing, Luxury etc)
- ✓ **Customer Service Skills**-Complaints Handling & Customer Retention
- ✓ **Debt Prevention & Collection Skills**
- ✓ **Etiquette & Grooming**
- ✓ **Leadership & Managerial Skills**
- ✓ **Self & Personal Development Skills**: Presentation Skills/ Effective Communication Skills/Business Proposal Writing Skills/ Problem Solving & Decision Making Skills/ Empowering Secretaries-The perfect PA! (For Secretaries & PA's)/ Effective Time Management/ Teamwork & Teambuilding/ P.R.I.D.E- **P**ersonal **R**esponsibility **I**n **D**elivering **E**xcellence